NATURAL LAW

PHILOSOPHY

Editor

PROFESSOR H. J. PATON,
M.A., F.B.A., D.LITT., LL.D.

*Emeritus Professor of Moral Philosophy
in the University of Oxford*

NATURAL LAW

An Introduction to Legal Philosophy

A. P. d'ENTRÈVES, M.A., D.PHIL.

*Professor of Government in the University of Turin
and formerly Serena Professor of Italian Studies in
the University of Oxford*

HUTCHINSON UNIVERSITY LIBRARY

LONDON

HUTCHINSON & CO. (Publishers) LTD
178-202 Great Portland Street, London, W.1

London Melbourne Sydney
Auckland Bombay Toronto
Johannesburg New York

★

First published 1951
Second impression 1952
Third impression 1955
Fourth impression 1957
Fifth impression 1960
Sixth impression 1961
Seventh impression 1963
Eighth impression 1964

Set in eleven point Imprint
and printed in Great Britain by
Fisher, Knight & Co. Ltd.
at the Gainsborough Press, St. Albans

CONTENTS

"It is odd, when one thinks of it, that there are people in the world who, having renounced all the laws of God and nature, have themselves made laws which they rigorously obey . . ."   *Pascal*

FOREWORD

THIS book is the outcome of eight lectures delivered at the University of Chicago in April 1948. I wish to thank the " Committee on Social Thought " and its Chairman, Professor J. U. Nef, for the opportunity they gave me to return to a subject which has been in my mind for many years. I also wish to thank the editor of this series, Professor H. J. Paton, for allowing me to state, in a concise and straightforward manner, my own very personal views and conclusions about the "nature of natural law". I wish further to thank him, as well as Professor D. A. Binchy, Mrs. I. Henderson and especially Mr. C. G. Hardie, for many helpful suggestions with regard to language and style.

Yet, on the point of releasing this short essay, I cannot avoid some misgivings. I am well aware that the language in which I have tried to express my thoughts is altogether a different one from that which prevails among present-day philosophers and political theorists. I am not sure that I have always succeeded in avoiding the over-emphasis which is the great temptation for a Latin. Above all, I have no claims to make as to the novelty of my material. The book is a good example of what supercilious scholars here in Oxford call "tertiary writing". The results of my own work in the field of legal and political philosophy I have published in a number of books and articles both in English and in my native Italian. I have had little scruple in drawing heavily upon them. But neither have I hesitated to avail myself of the conclusions of better scholars than I am, wherever they seemed to me to carry weight and final authority. What little originality the book may possess must therefore lie in the statement of a case rather than in the production of the evidence. That case may or may not be accepted. It is my hope that I may at least have succeeded in making it worth hearing.

To account for the themes that have inspired me would require a separate volume. I have no doubt that they will be sufficiently apparent to the attentive reader. I would like to recall in this connection my lasting attachment to the Law Faculty of my old University in Turin, where I received my first training *in utroque iure*, as well as in that *vera non simulata philosophia* which has remained an essential part of a great legal tradition. But, if so short an essay allowed of a dedication, I would not hesitate to inscribe it to the memory of many a friend of later and darker days, whose deeds bear witness to the existence of the Law which alone deserves ultimate allegiance.

Oxford, March 1950.

In revising this book for its first reprint, I have not been able to make more than a few corrections and additions to the text. Most of these have been suggested by readers and reviewers—and there have been friends and foes among them. I have taken care to meet the complaints of my critic in "Mind" regarding the initials of the authors cited in the bibliographies; but I have made no attempt to better what he calls my "elusive prose". As I pointed out in the Foreword, I was well aware that to many my language would seem "ambiguous" and obsolete.

Since this essay was written, however, I have come across a sentence by the editor of "Mind" which I would like to quote here at length, not only as an example of the language which I have so far been unable to master, but also as conveying a thought which (if I understand it correctly) is not very dissimilar from that which forms the main contention of this book.

"Ethical statements," writes Professor Ryle in *The Concept of Mind*, "as distinct from particular *ad hominem* behests and reproaches, should be regarded as warrants addressed to any potential givers of behests and reproaches, i.e. not as personal action-tickets but as impersonal injunction-tickets; not imperatives but 'laws' that only such things as imperatives and punishments can satisfy. Like statute laws they are to be construed not as orders, but as licences to give and enforce orders."

I am not sure that I would meet the objections of my critic and make my argument more clear and convincing if I now hinted that my own notion of law somewhat corresponds to Professor Ryle's "personal action-tickets" and my notion of morals to his "impersonal injunction-tickets". But I am sure that the distinction to which Professor Ryle lends the weight of his authority—viz. that it is a different thing "to give and enforce orders", and to provide a "licence" for doing so—is one which will make the old natural law theorists rejoice in their graves. "Laws" that are not "imperatives" but "warrants" for "potential givers of behests and reproaches" seem to me to bear less resemblance to statute laws than to the "natural law" that fills so many volumes now lying dusty and neglected on the shelves of our libraries.

Oxford, May 1952

INTRODUCTION

For over two thousand years the idea of natural law has played a prominent part in thought and in history. It was conceived as the ultimate measure of right and wrong, as the pattern of the good life or "life according to nature". It provided a potent incentive to reflection, the touchstone of existing institutions, the justification of conservatism as well as of revolution. But recourse to natural law was never entirely unchallenged. The notion was laden with ambiguity even in the days when it was considered self-evident. In the last century and a half it has been assailed from many sides as critically unsound and as historically pernicious. It was declared to be dead, never to rise again from its ashes. Yet natural law has survived and still calls for discussion. It is the purpose of this book to examine the reasons for that vitality and the claim of natural law to have served the cause of humanity well.

But how is natural law best approached and how should it be handled ? This is a serious difficulty to the modern student. There is no doubt that, for a number of reasons, we have grown unfamiliar with the whole body of doctrine and with its terminology. We find ourselves confronted with a variety of definitions, and we can see no reason why we should make our start from one rather than from another. There is, however, one important restriction which must be laid down from the outset, to circumscribe the ground which this book proposes to cover. The notion of natural law which it discusses is a notion which refers to human behaviour, not to physical phenomena. Our concern is with ethics and politics, not with the natural sciences. The word *nature* is the cause of the equivocation. The failure to distinguish clearly between its different meanings was the source of all the ambiguities in the doctrine of natural law.[1]

Prima facie, there seem to be two possible lines of approach to our subject. I would call the one historical, the other philo-

[1] For an analysis of the notion of the law of nature in scientific thought see A. N. WHITEHEAD, *Adventures of Ideas*, 1935, chapter vii.

sophical. We may consider the doctrine of natural law as an historical product. A recurrent motif in Western thought and history, we may attempt to retrace its development and to stress its importance in shaping the destinies of the West—and our own. But we may, on the other hand, consider natural law as a philosophical doctrine. An ideal or a deception, it claims to have a value which is not merely historical, but universal. It can be stressed as a positive or negative contribution to man's knowledge of himself and of his place in the universe.

Neither line of approach seems entirely satisfactory. Not the historical, because a history of natural law is a formidable undertaking, however confidently eminent scholars may have thought and felt about it. "The Law of Nature has a perfectly continuous history," wrote Sir Frederick Pollock in an admirable little essay on *The History of the Law of Nature*. This view was accepted and emphasized by almost all modern historians of political thought. They have all stressed, and rightly, the tenacity with which natural law terminology has held its ground in ethics and politics ever since the Greeks first coined it at the dawn of our civilization. A quotation from Sir Ernest Barker's recent book, *Traditions of Civility*, will provide a good illustration of the manner in which the process is viewed by one of the greatest English students of the subject :

> " The origin of the idea of natural law may be ascribed to an old and indefeasible movement of the human mind (we may trace it already in the *Antigone* of Sophocles) which impels it towards the notion of an eternal and immutable justice ; a justice which human authority expresses, or ought to express—but does not make ; a justice which human authority may fail to express—and must pay the penalty for failing to express by the diminution, or even the forfeiture, of its power to command. This justice is conceived as being the higher or ultimate law, proceeding from the nature of the universe—from the Being of God and the reason of man. It follows that law—in the sense of the law of the last resort—is somehow above law-making. It follows that lawmakers, after all, are somehow under and subject to law.
>
> " The movement of the mind of man towards these conceptions and their consequences is already apparent in the *Ethics*

and the *Rhetoric* of Aristotle. But it was among the Stoic thinkers of the Hellenistic age that the movement first attained a large and general expression ; and that expression . . . became a tradition of human civility which runs continuously from the Stoic teachers of the Porch to the American Revolution of 1776 and the French Revolution of 1789. Allied to theology for many centuries—adopted by the Catholic Church, and forming part of the general teaching of the Schoolmen and the Canonists—the theory of Natural Law had become in the sixteenth century, and continued to remain during the seventeenth and the eighteenth, an independent and rationalist system, professed and expounded by the philosophers of the secular school of natural law."

This is a grandiose picture, but it leaves out many details and raises more questions than it purports to solve. Surely the mere fact that an identical expression recurs in different writers is no proof of the continuity of thought from one to the other. That Cicero and Locke should both have defined natural law in a very similar manner is no evidence of the uninterrupted acceptance of that notion during the eighteen odd centuries which separate them. The philosophers of the "secular school," to whom Sir Ernest Barker refers, would probably have denied the continuity which he outlines so effectively. They had different views from ours about the losses which the "dark ages" inflicted upon mankind. They would have denounced Schoolmen and Canonists alike for obscuring the true doctrine of natural law which they claimed to restore to its purity.[1] Except for the name, the medieval and the modern notions of natural law have little in common.

This is the sort of difficulty which we would certainly encounter if we were ever to entertain the ambitious programme of writing a history of natural law. It is a difficulty inherent in the history of political ideas, perhaps in *Ideengeschichte* altogether. What I have said of natural law can be said of other famous political concepts, such as the social contract or democracy. There can be no greater delusion than to believe that the history of these notions may be written by simply

---

[1] This point was significantly stressed by Pufendorf, the most celebrated and influential of all seventeenth century writers on natural law.

drawing up a list, as careful and complete as possible, of all the references to them which can be found in political writers. The formal continuity of certain expressions is not the decisive factor : the same notion may have had very different meanings and have served entirely different purposes. The history of ideas is an internal history ; it is from within, not from without that the value of a doctrine must be assessed—as when new wine is poured into old bottles, it is the new wine that matters and sometimes causes the old bottle to burst.

I remember that Dr. A. J. Carlyle used to say that there is very little that is really new in political theory.   Men have kept repeating the old slogans over and over again.   The novelty is very often only a question of accent.   Democracy, Social Contract, Natural Law may well be traced back to the Greeks. But Aristotle's notion of democracy is not that of Jefferson ; nor does the fact that the Sophists came very near the idea of a social contract give us much help to a better understanding of Rousseau.   As far as natural law is concerned, it was Lord Bryce who remarked that, at a given moment, "that which had been for nearly two thousand years a harmless maxim, almost a commonplace of morality," was converted into "a mass of dynamite which shattered an ancient monarchy and shook the European continent."   We should not pretend to know much about natural law unless we are able to solve this historical riddle.

What I have called the philosophical approach brings us undoubtedly much nearer the answer.   I have already noted that many of the ambiguities of the concept of natural law must be ascribed to the ambiguity of the concept of nature that underlies it.   But it is not enough to point out that, notwithstanding the similar words which are used to denote them, the notion of natural law which has played so prominent a part in ethics and politics is something intrinsically different from the notion of the law of nature which is elaborated by the scientist.   It is necessary further to account both for the similarity and for the difference.

Now it is easy enough to understand the reason which prompted men to indicate by a similar name the measure of their actions and the rules that govern a reality which escapes

their control.   It is the quest after some immutable standard
or pattern, independent of their choice and capable of carrying
conviction.   The contrast between "nature" and "convention"
is only one aspect of a deeper antithesis. As Pascal pointed out,
it may well be that "nature" is but a "first custom", as custom
is a "second nature".[1]   What matters is the constant endeavour
to place certain principles beyond discussion, by raising them to
a different plane altogether.   The nature-metaphor was
admirably fitted to express the notion of finality and inevitability.   It is a curious paradox that this same metaphor
should also have been used to indicate a task or a duty.   The
concept of nature was a double-edged sword which could be
employed in two opposite directions.

It was not only double-edged.   It was flexible.   Nature
could have widely different meanings.   We cannot fail to be
aware of that difference when we read two sentences like "man
is by nature a political animal" and "men are by nature equal
and free".   The different meanings of natural law are but the
consequences of the different meanings of nature.   Professor
Ritchie, himself a declared enemy of natural law, saw this point
very clearly in his old but still valuable book on *Natural Rights*.
He pointed out that the history of the law of nature is really
nothing else than the history of the idea of nature in law and
in politics.   He therefore attempted to clarify, under different
headings, the principal usages of the word "nature" in political
science, and gave this section of his book the significant title
De Divisione Naturae.

I think that this is, on the whole, a much more satisfactory
approach to the problem of natural law than the purely
historical one.   For one thing it accounts for the fact that there
is really not one tradition of natural law, but many.   The
medieval and the modern conceptions of natural law are two
different doctrines ;   the continuity between them is mainly
a question of words.   The philosophical approach also allows
for the grouping of different authors on deeper than mere
chronological grounds.   If Cicero and Locke agree in their
definition of natural law, this is an indication of a more intimate

[1] " J'ai grand peur que cette nature ne soit elle-même qu'une première
coutume, comme la coutume est une seconde nature" (*Pensées*, II, 93).

link than mere imitation or repetition. Finally, only philosophy can provide the clue to the problems which history lays bare but is unable to solve. If the modern doctrine of natural law proved to be so different from the old both in its implications and in its far-reaching consequences, the reason is that a new conception of man and the universe turned what had been for centuries a harmless and orthodox doctrine into a potent instrument of progress and revolution, which gave an entirely new turn to history and of which we still feel the effects.

There is, however, one serious objection to this manner of handling our subject. Classifications are open to question. They vary according to the conceptions or preconceptions that underlie them. They are very often mere window-dressing for superficial thought. There is no end to the divisions and subdivisions required to cover and to account for the infinite varieties of natural law. And these in turn provide arguments for the sceptical denial of natural law as one of the great deceptions of ethics. "The word *natural*," wrote Hume, "is commonly taken in so many senses, and is of so loose a signification, that it seems vain to dispute whether justice be natural or not." It would indeed be lamentable if, having approached natural law from the angle of philosophy, we found ourselves pursuing a will-o'-the-wisp. It is good that history should remind us that this highly controversial doctrine was after all one of the most creative forces, one of the most constructive elements of our culture and of our civilization.

I can see only one way out of the difficulties which I have outlined and stressed so far. It is to combine history and philosophy in the study of what I have already called the vitality of natural law and its claim to have served the cause of humanity well. In my opinion what really calls for attention on the part of the modern student is the function of natural law rather than the doctrine itself, the issues that lay behind it rather than the controversies about its essence. "In order to understand the dominance of natural law we must interpret it psychologically, and therefore relate it to the forces that operated through its medium." I think that we should take as our guide this pregnant remark of a great student of history and of philosophy.[1] We must try to see through the abstract and academic façade of natural law. We must endeavour to understand the causes of its constant recurrence. Surely an undertaking of this kind calls for historical as well as for philosophical assistance.

I shall not attempt in this book to sketch a history, however condensed, of the doctrine of natural law. I shall concentrate on its merits. I have therefore chosen what seemed to me the best illustrations of the part which that doctrine has played in the course of our history. But for natural law the petty laws of a small peasant community of peninsular Italy would never have become the universal law of an international civilization. But for natural law the great medieval synthesis of godly and of worldly wisdom would not have been possible. But for natural law there would probably have been no American and no French revolution, nor would the great ideals of freedom and equality have found their way into the law-books after having found it into the hearts of men. These three major events provide the substance of the three first chapters of this book. They will certainly need to be revised and implemented by the professional historian.

When we come to our present situation the line of approach must necessarily vary. The author of this study has no particular axe to grind in favour of one notion of natural law or another. He cannot help wondering at the ingenuity with which certain authors still contrive to draw up elaborate treatises on "natural law and the rights of man" in an age which has grown so sceptical about absolute and immutable values, so hostile to the spirit of hope and optimism which inspired that doctrine in its heyday and ensured its success. But he cannot help feeling that the case for natural law is not usually put forward with the necessary fairness. He would like to draw attention to the fact that, though the terminology has gone and little seems left of natural law thinking in modern jurisprudence and politics, many of the points which are generally accepted as the first elements of those "sciences" are really nothing else than the points which were traditionally discussed under the heading of natural law.

[1] See note at the end of this chapter.

The essence of law, the delimitation of its province, the conditions of its validity, were problems long known to the student before the invention of positive jurisprudence and political science. They survive, *mutato nomine*, in the text-books of academic teaching. Present-day lawyers and politicians may scorn their benighted forebears. They may declare that they have nothing to do with natural law nor with the ideals which it represented. But they have not succeeded in eliminating the problems which natural law purported to solve. They cannot fail to be faced by these problems the moment they begin to reflect on the results of their labours and on the safety of the ground which they tread.

We have indeed done little more than give a new name to a very old thing. We say that these problems are the domain of legal and political philosophy. I think that legal and political philosophy are nothing else than natural law writ large. And I earnestly hope that I may succeed in the last three chapters of this book in making this statement less paradoxical. That there may be some scope for a re-examination of the problem is after all the tacit assumption which underlies the inclusion of a book on natural law in a series on the main problems of philosophy.

NOTE.—I know of only one author who has followed on the lines suggested in the words of Dilthey, which I have quoted on p. 12 of this Introduction. E. Troeltsch was not merely a student of history, but a trained philosopher and theologian. He was thus admirably equipped to survey the complex interplay of forces and ideas which resulted in the formation of European culture. Some of his works have been translated into English, and I wish to refer to them as the best and most stimulating treatment of the problem of natural law from the point of view both of philosophy and of history. It is significant that Troeltsch should never have claimed for his conclusions anything more than a provisional value. He conceived them as a personal contribution towards a better understanding of our spiritual heritage.

He began by outlining the function of natural law in the development of Christian ethics (*The Social Teaching of the Christian Churches*, 1912—transl. by O. Wyon, 2 vols., New York, 1931). Natural law, he pointed out, meant the intrusion of an alien element in Christianity. It represented the inheritance of the ancient world which could be adapted to

Christian teaching.   It provided the basis for a social and political programme which was entirely lacking in the Gospel.   The variations of natural law between the two extremes of rationalism and irrationalism accounted in his view for the different attitude of the Christian Churches towards the " outer world ", and for the variations of their social and political doctrines.   The great contrast between the Catholic and the Protestant views on such matters could be reduced, according to Troeltsch, to a fundamental difference in the manner of conceiving the powers and duties of man as expressed in the law of nature.

Later, under the impact of the First World War and of the defeat of his country, Troeltsch was led to recast his views in a new and different pattern.   In his lecture on *The Idea of Natural Law and Humanity* (1922), he put forward an even more dramatic explanation of the contrasts which divided Europe.   The belief in natural law, both as a recognition of a law common to humanity and as an assertion of the fundamental rights of man, was, he pointed out, the distinguishing mark of political thought in Western Europe.   From that belief the German world had broken away in the age of Romanticism, perhaps indeed at an earlier date still.   From that time onwards German thought had been drifting towards the glorification of force over reason and of the State as the supreme embodiment of moral life.

As Sir Ernest Barker has remarked, the contrast drawn by Troeltsch between German thought and the thought of Western Europe is a contrast which can be accepted only with many qualifications.   But, as I have already said, Troeltsch never considered his interpretations as final.   It is useless to speculate how he would have recast them had he lived to witness the ideological conflict of the Second World War and that of present-day Europe. The sweeping advance of Marxism would probably have made him aware of the fallacy of linking theoretical attitudes to racial or national characters.   But he would not have hesitated, I think, to maintain that it is no use opposing the old doctrine of natural law to the challenge of the economic interpretation of history without reviving the spirit which found in that doctrine its verbal expression.

GENERAL LITERATURE

SIR H. S. MAINE, *Ancient Law*, 1861, Chapters iii and iv.

D. G. RITCHIE, *Natural Rights*, 1895, P. i, Chapters i-iv.

SIR J. W. SALMOND, *The Law of Nature*, in "Law Quarterly Review," 1895.

SIR F. POLLOCK, *The History of the Law of Nature*, 1900, in *Essays in the Law*, 1922.

LORD BRYCE, *The Law of Nature*, in *Studies in History and Jurisprudence*, Vol. II, 1901.

E. TROELTSCH, *The Ideas of Natural Law and Humanity in Western Politics*, 1922 (Appendix I to GIERKE—BARKER, *Natural Law and the Theory of Society*).

J. DEWEY, *Nature and Reason in Law*, in *Philosophy and Civilisation*, 1931.

SIR E. BARKER, Introduction to GIERKE, *Natural Law and the Theory of Society*, 1934.

J. W. JONES, *Historical Introduction to the Theory of Law*, 1940, Chapter iv, *The Law of Nature*.

H. ROMMEN, *The Natural Law*, transl. by T. R. Hanley, 1947.

A German work by J. SAUTER, *Die philosophischen Grundlagen des Naturrechts*, 1932, deserves to be mentioned.

General works on the history of political theory, such as HILDEBRAND, REHM, JANET, DUNNING, CARLYLE, MCILWAIN, DOYLE, SABINE and others, should be consulted.

A useful selection of texts will be found in J. HALL, *Readings in Jurisprudence*, Chapter i.

A UNIVERSAL SYSTEM OF LAWS

THE first great achievement of natural law lies in the legal field proper, in the foundation, that is, of a system of laws of universal validity. That system was embodied and transmitted to posterity in the law-books of Justinian.

It is no exaggeration to say that, next to the Bible, no book has left a deeper mark upon the history of mankind than the *Corpus Iuris Civilis*. Much has been written about the impact of Rome upon Western civilization. Much has been disputed about "the ghost of the Roman Empire" that still lurks far beyond the shores of the Mediterranean. The heritage of Roman law is not a ghost, but a living reality. It is present in the court as well as in the market-place. It lives on not only in the institutions but even in the language of all civilized nations.

To the pessimist or the sceptic, who too readily accepts the view that ideologies are nothing but a superstructure on facts, the history of that heritage is a reminder of the predominance of the spiritual over the material factor. "The history of Roman Law during the Middle Ages testifies to the latent vigour and organizing power of ideas in the midst of shifting surroundings" (Vinogradoff). The revival of Roman law was a powerful leaven in the transformation of the social and political structure of Europe. Those who speak of a *damnosa hereditas* have their eye only on one side of the picture. They overlook what is our greatest debt to the Roman inheritance : the notion that law is the common patrimony of men, a bond that can overcome their differences and reduce them to unity.

The great compilation and codification of legal material which is commonly known by the name of the *Corpus Iuris Civilis*, was completed in the year 534 A.D. by a body of Byzantine lawyers who had been ordered to undertake that task by the Emperor Justinian. It embodied the results of a long

and complex development which had begun in the fifth century
B.C. with the first written laws of the Romans, the *Twelve
Tables*. For many centuries to come Roman law was identified
with "the godly approved laws of Justinian the Emperor".
The mature fruit obscured the process by which the fruit had
been ripened.[1]

It is only in comparatively recent times that Roman law has
begun to be treated "historically". Modern scholars are
engaged in painstaking efforts to disentangle the "classical"
element from the Byzantine additions and modifications. But
in the eyes of posterity it was Justinian's greatness to have
given the laws simplicity and symmetry. Dante reserved a
special place in Paradise to the Byzantine Cæsar :

> "Who by the will of Primal Love possessed
> Pruned from the Laws the unneeded and the vain."
> (*Paradiso*, vi, 11-12. Binyon's transl.)

What impressed later generations, besides the admirable
construction of Justinian's law-books, was their claim to
universal validity. Little heed was paid to the fact that those
books had been compiled in the East, and at a time when the
power of Rome had ceased to hold sway in Western Europe.
Nor for a time did their composite structure disturb the student
with questions of authenticity or "interpolations". Our medieval ancestors were perhaps more appreciative than we are of that
Byzantine art of the mosaic, to which the *Corpus Iuris* offers a
striking parallel. But their historical judgment was after all
not entirely inaccurate. It was through her law that Rome
reconquered the provinces which she had lost on the battlefield.

Now there is one point about that claim to validity which
should not fail to impress even the modern and unprejudiced
reader. That claim was not based on force, but on reason.
It was an appeal to the intrinsic dignity of the law, rather than
to its power of compulsion. In a resounding proclamation
(Const. "Deo Auctore") Justinian declared that it had been his

---

[1] The *Corpus Iuris Civilis* comprises three different works : the *Institutes*,
a short educational handbook, published in Nov. 533 ; the *Digest*, a collection of excerpts or fragments from earlier jurists systematically arranged
(publ. Dec. 533) ; and the *Codex* or codification of Imperial constitutions,
first published in 520, and revised in Nov. 534.

purpose to erect a temple to Justice, a citadel of Law. "Of all subjects none is more worthy of study than the authority of Laws, which happily disposes things divine and human, and puts an end to iniquity."

This idea is taken up and expanded in the opening paragraphs of the *Digest*, where the views of the more famous Roman jurists on the subject are quoted (*Dig.*, liber I, titulus I, *De Iustitia et Iure*). Law—*Ius*—is an art and a science all in one.[1] As a science, it is a knowledge of human and divine things (*divinarum atque humanarum rerum notitia*), a theory of right and wrong (*iusti atque iniusti scientia*). As an art, it is the furtherance of what is good and equitable (*ars boni et aequi*). So high is the mission of the jurist that it may rightly be compared with that of a priest (*merito quis nos sacerdotes appellet*). He is indeed a minister of justice, for justice and law are correlative (*iustitia est constans et perpetua voluntas ius suum cuique tribuere*).

Now of laws there are different sorts. There is the law of the State, which expresses the interest of one particular community (*ius civile*). There is a law of nations (*ius gentium*), which men have devised for their mutual intercourse. But there is also a law which expresses a higher and more permanent standard. It is the law of nature (*ius naturale*), which corresponds to "that which is always good and equitable" (*bonum et aequum*).

I have summarized and condensed what to the scholar is an object of hair-splitting controversy. Every single word in this first chapter of the *Digest* has been weighed and contested. What liberties did the Byzantine compilers take with the texts they were quoting? Is the fundamental distinction between the three categories of law (*ius civile, ius gentium, ius naturale*) a "classical" Roman conception, or is it a later invention? How can we account for the contradictions which are still apparent between the very authors who are bundled together under the heading *De Iustitia et Iure*? What, behind their rhetorical appeal, is the exact meaning and the real source of such words and concepts as *naturale, aequum et bonum* and

[1] On the different meanings of the Latin word *ius*, and the difficulty of giving its correct English equivalent. see below, pp. 59-60.

others ? It is difficult to say whether there is more cause to take pride or to complain that, after more than a hundred years of historical studies, large sections of the *Corpus Iuris* have become a quagmire, or rather a minefield, for the inexperienced reader.

I think, however, that we should not hesitate to read the opening paragraphs of the *Digest* with the candour of the inexperienced. It is after all the only way we have to try and represent to ourselves the impression that they must have conveyed to generation after generation of students who turned to the *Corpus Iuris* for apprenticeship in the law, and who took its words at their face value. The impression in approaching the temple or citadel of law must have been enhanced rather than diminished by that rhetorical opening—Byzantine or genuinely Roman as the texts may be. Here was a system of laws which purported to fulfil the highest aspirations of men and their needs in all circumstances. The edifice was grandiose enough, and the archway leading to it proportionate to its grandeur. Natural law was its key-stone. No wonder that it should have focussed admiration and attention.

But on the part of the modern student both admiration and attention must be qualified and critical. We are confronted with a problem of interpretation exactly on the lines which have been discussed in the Introduction. Let me recall briefly how the Roman doctrine of natural law is usually viewed by historians and political philosophers. The origin of that doctrine, it is pointed out and correctly, was certainly not Roman. It was a foreign importation. It was borrowed wholesale from Greek philosophy, particularly from Stoicism. Stoic doctrine inspired the definition of Cicero, a good representative of the fashionable eclecticism which prevailed among the Roman well-to-do in the last century before our era.

"True law is right reason in agreement with Nature; it is of universal application, unchanging and everlasting ; it summons to duty by its commands, and averts from wrong-doing by its prohibitions. And it does not lay its commands or prohibitions upon good men in vain, though neither have any effect on the wicked. It is a sin to try to alter this law, nor is it allowable to attempt to repeal any part of it, and it is impossible to abolish it entirely. We cannot be freed from its obligations by Senate or People, and we need not look outside ourselves for an expounder or interpreter of it. And there will not be different laws at Rome and at Athens, or different laws now and in the future, but one eternal and unchangeable law will be valid for all nations and for all times, and there will be one master and one ruler, that is, God, over us all, for He is the author of this law, its promulgator, and its enforcing judge " (*De Republica*, III, xxii, 33).

This famous passage from Cicero's *Republic* clearly sets forth the doctrine of the law of nature which had been elaborated by the Stoics. Mankind is a universal community or cosmopolis. Law is its expression. Being based upon the common nature of men, it is truly universal. Being endorsed by the sovereign Lordship of God, it is eternal and immutable. The doctrine passed into the *ius naturale* of the Roman jurists as well as into the teaching of the Christian Church. It is significant that Cicero's definition should have been preserved for us by a Christian writer, Lactantius. It is not surprising that Justinian, the Christian law-giver, should have taken the idea of natural law as the corner-stone of his system. It could be supported and implemented by the authority of the jurists who are quoted in the *Digest* as referring to *ius naturale* as the ultimate principle underlying all legal differences, and as the infallible means of reducing those differences to unity.

A similar continuity of thought is usually traced also in a number of concepts closely correlated to the doctrine of natural law. First and foremost the concept of equality. Cicero, following the Stoics on this point also, had clearly formulated the notion of the fundamental equality of all men.

"No single thing is so like another, so exactly its counterpart, as all of us are to one another. Nay, if bad habits and false beliefs did not twist the weaker minds and turn them in whatever direction they are inclined, no one would be so like his own self as all men would be like all others. And so, however we may define man, a single definition will apply to all . . . For those creatures who have received the gift of reason from Nature have also received right reason, and therefore they have also received the gift of Law, which is right reason applied to command and prohibition. And if they have received law, they have received Justice also. Now all men have received reason; therefore all men have received justice " (*De Legibus*, I, x, 29 ; xii, 33).

The notion that men are equal is here deduced from the very existence of a bond that unites them. Human equality is the direct consequence of natural law, its first and essential tenet. This doctrine, which Dr. Carlyle defined as the dividing line between ancient and modern political theory, was admirably traced by him down to the Roman jurists—and far beyond. Cicero's sweeping generalisations about the nature of man and the dictates of the law of nature recur in Seneca and are the foundation of the dogmatic statements of the lawyers in the *Corpus Iuris*. "We are indeed at the beginning of a theory of human nature and society of which the 'Liberty, Equality and Fraternity' of the French Revolution is only the present-day expression."

Lastly, according to modern interpreters, one common mark of the doctrine of natural law from Cicero to Justinian is a particular attitude to the social and political problem. Here again we must turn for the sources of that attitude to the Greeks rather than to the Romans. It is the idea of a difference or contrast between the ideal pattern of society which is expressed by the law of nature, and the positive legal institutions which confront us in the reality of human interrelations.

This idea can be retraced in Cicero's definition, which I have just quoted. It is implicit in the reference to the laws of Rome and of Athens, of the present and of the future, as contrasting with the eternal and unchangeable law of God and of Nature. It is further enlarged where the fundamental equality of men is contrasted with their actual inequalities, and these are attributed to the impact of "bad habits and false beliefs". The notion of natural law clearly refers to that contrast between "nature" and "convention," between φύσις and νόμος, which played so great a part in Greek philosophy and in Greek political thought. That contrast had provided the Sophists with the most powerful weapon for their criticism of existing institutions. It had been successfully met by Plato and Aristotle in their discussion of human nature in politics.

It was revived in the Stoic gospel of cosmopolitanism and of a "return to nature." It is characteristic of Cicero that he should not have drawn all the implications which the contrast implied. But later writers, such as Seneca, were to develop them more fully. And the distinction between the natural and the conventional is the very backbone of the theory of law which is laid down in the *Corpus Iuris Civilis*.

Thus do modern historians and political philosophers tend to attribute a paramount importance to the philosophical element underlying that theory. A further confirmation of that importance is derived from the very opening of the *Digest*, where it is said that the jurist, in order to be a minister of justice, must also be a follower of "true philosophy." The great jurists of the golden age of Roman law, says a recent historian (Rommen), were for the most part also philosophers. Under the influence of Stoic philosophy the doctrine of natural law passed into Roman law—to be handed on to later thought. Justinian's law-books afford the confirmation of the "perfectly continuous history" of that doctrine.

Now it may seem impertinent to raise doubts on what is still the current and commonly accepted interpretation. But it is impossible not to do so when the evidence is more closely examined. For one thing, it is highly perplexing to find that modern students of Roman law take a very different view of the matter.

According to them, the Roman jurists were a singularly unphilosophical breed of men. They were a professional class, and far-reaching speculations (such as Cicero's) about the ideal law or the ultimate nature of justice were not properly within the range of their interest. They may have availed themselves of Greek philosophical notions, but legal philosophy never developed among them. This applies not only to the jurists of the Republican period, the period when Greek influences and modes of thought were beginning to sweep the Roman world. It applies also to the "classical" period, which stretches from Augustus to Diocletian, the great creative period of Roman law and Roman jurisprudence.

Whatever occasional references can be found in the writings of the jurists to the problem of justice, or to the nature of

jurisprudence, or to natural law, should therefore be treated
with the greatest suspicion. They should be considered as
possible reminiscences of class-room teaching, or as ornamental commonplaces not to be taken too seriously. Or the
words may have a technical meaning which can be only
obscured by referring them to philosophical currents and
influences. Finally, allowance must be made in all cases for
post-classical insertions and additions.

Such warnings as these make us realize the importance
of what I have called the painstaking efforts of scholars to
ascertain the authenticity of the texts which were transmitted to us by Justinian. They make us aware that the
high-sounding phrases which are set forth in the opening
paragraphs of the *Digest*—and above all the notion of *ius
naturale*—conceal the most complex and difficult problems of
interpretation. Clearly, our views about the continuity and
importance of the natural law tradition cannot fail to be
seriously affected if it is proved that all references to it are
but rhetorical ornaments of doubtful attribution.

But there is no need to be a specialist in Roman law to feel
uneasy about the definition of *ius naturale*. It is indeed very
difficult to construct a coherent doctrine from the different
views which are expressed on the subject in the passages
quoted in the *Digest*. These views appear to contradict one
another to an extent which cannot fail to impress even such
readers who are unaware of the most up-to-date results of
textual criticism. The most characteristic contradiction is that
which concerns the relations between natural law (*ius naturale*),
the civil law (*ius civile*) and the law of nations (*ius gentium*).

There is no doubt that, in the lawyers whose authority is
referred to by Justinian, we find not one but several different
views on the matter. Here are the passages which best illus-
trate this contradiction. The first is given under the name of
Ulpian, a jurist of the age of Alexander Severus (first half of
the third century A.D.). It is allegedly derived from his
book of *Institutes*, a work which has unfortunately been lost ;
indeed, its very existence has been doubted by scholars.
The passage runs as follow :

Dig., I, i, 1 (*ULPIANUS libro primo institutionum*): "Private law is threefold ; it can be gathered from the precepts of nature, or from those of the nations, or from those of the city. Natural law is that which nature has taught all animals ; this law indeed is not peculiar to the human race, but belongs to all animals . . . From this law springs the union of male and female, which we call matrimony, the procreation of children and their education . . . The law of nations is that law which mankind observes. It is easy to understand that this law should differ from the natural, inasmuch as the latter belongs to all animals, while the former is peculiar to men."

A few paragraphs below this quotation from Ulpian we read one from Gaius, a jurist of an earlier generation. It is taken from his book of *Institutes*, the only classical work which has come down to us in anything like its original state, and which is usually dated 161 A.D. There can therefore be little doubt about the authenticity of the text as given in the *Digest :*

Dig., I, i, 9 (*GAIUS libro primo institutionum*) : "All peoples who are governed by law and by custom observe laws which in part are their own and in part are common to all mankind. For those laws which each people has given itself are peculiar to each city and are called the civil law (*ius civile*) . . . But what natural reason dictates to all men and is most equally observed among them is called the law of nations, as that law which is practised by all mankind."

Only a few paragraphs further on, we find the definition of Paulus, a contemporary of Ulpian's :

Dig., I, i, 11 (*PAULUS libro quarto decimo ad Sabinum*) : "We can speak of law in different senses ; in one sense, when we call law what is always equitable and good, as is natural law. In another sense, what in each city is profitable to all or to many, as is civil law (*ius civile*)."

The divergencies between these three passages are obvious. Ulpian lays down a tripartite division of law ; Gaius and Paulus a twofold one. Ulpian sharply asserts the difference between natural law and the other human laws ; Gaius the identity of the dictates of natural reason with the law of nations. Finally, Ulpian conceives of natural law as something like the general instinct of animals ; while Gaius and Paulus see the reason for the universal validity of certain principles in

their rational character and in their acceptance by all mankin
as well as in their inherent utility and goodness.

The difference between these quite opposite ways
approaching the problem of the ultimate foundation of la
is further apparent from many other passages referring
natural law, both in the first chapter of the *Digest* and elsewher
The jurists from whom the Byzantine compilers derived the
authorities seem to fall into two groups.

On one side, Ulpian himself, and several other author
clearly oppose the *ius gentium* to the *ius naturale* or to natur
They seem to conceive of all men as having been born fr
and equal, bound only by the ties of family relationship, an
with an equal right to such things as by natural law are th
common patrimony of mankind. One of the jurists of a sti
later date, Hermogenianus (fourth century A.D.), is quoted a
giving a list of the institutions which come under the *iu
gentium*; among them are wars, the separation of nations, th
foundation of kingdoms, the division of property, in short, a
those legal and political institutions which have developed ou
of the growing complexity of human intercourse and life. I
is not said explicitly of these institutions, as it is said of slavery
that they are against nature; but the assumption is clearl
that they do not correspond to natural law, and the inspirin
motive is a contrast between nature and convention.

Gaius, on the other hand, seems to stand alone in main
taining that the institutions of the law of nations can b
rationally justified, inasmuch as men have been led by "natura
reason" to adopt them.

I have tried to sum up as briefly as possible the difficultie
which the doctrine of natural law, as it is laid down in th
Digest, presents to the reader. I have no intention of discussin
in detail the many explanations which have been proposed ir
order to solve these difficulties.

The easiest and most obvious explanation is a historical one
The literature which was used and condensed by order o
Justinian, it is pointed out, covers a range of several centuries
Such an extent of time may well account for a change of min
and of attitude. The different views which appear to hav
been held by the writers of different periods might thus b

eferred to the impact of different schools of thought, perhaps also to the growth of a new conception of life which was to nd its full expression in Christianity.

More radically, many among the most authoritative tudents of Roman law have suggested that all the general efinitions which are contained in the text of the *Digest* hould be considered as dubious. When they were not ctually the result of direct interpolation by the Byzantines, hese definitions are at any rate—as has already been said— urely ornamental and devoid of any juridical value. In articular, Ulpian's definition of natural law—that unlucky hrase, as Sir Frederick Pollock termed it, entirely alien to the egal tradition (Jolowicz) as well as contrary to the Stoic onception of the law of nature (Schulz)—is now usually onsidered a post-classical insertion ; and so is the trichotomy *us civile, ius gentium, ius naturale*, as opposed to the dichotomy *us civile, ius gentium* (= *ius naturale*). All the blame would then est with the Byzantine compilers. They had been ordered y Justinian to omit, and even to alter, "everything in the ncient books that ye shall find badly stated, or superfluous, r imperfect" (Const. "Deo Auctore"). They made the issues nly more obscure in their endeavour *de solliciter doucement es textes* . . .

Such explanations and suggestions carry weight, coming, s they do, from most authoritative quarters. But they lo not account for one fact, which impresses itself upon the eader of the *Digest* the moment he forgets the quarrel about he classical and post-classical elements that went into its omposition. If there are many contradictions between the exts, surely the Byzantine compilers must have been aware of hem. And since they had authority to remove them, why lid they not do so ? How can it be explained that they should ave welded together a number of contradictory authorities, in he deliberate attempt to prefix to their compilation a section lealing with the highest problems of law, *De Iustitia et Iure* ? think that we should fix our attention on the common lements which that section contains rather than on its contra- lictions.

Let us go back for a moment to that claim to universal

validity which, in the eyes of posterity, constituted the greates
appeal of Justinian's law-books and which was so prominentl
in the mind of their author. The foundation of that universa
validity purported to be a rational foundation. It could b
provided only by an absolute standard of justice. This standar
is *ius naturale*. In the *Digest*, Ulpian's "natural instinct
could suffice to prove that there are certain institutions whic
are inherent in all animal life. The universality of law i
pegged to nature in its broadest sense. In the *Institutes*, wher
the Christian Emperor speaks out in his own name, the existenc
of natural law is attributed to a will superior to that of an
law-giver. "The laws of nature, which are most equall
observed by all nations, remain always stable and immutabl
enacted as they are by some kind of divine providence (*Inst.
I, ii, 11).

But along with the principles which can be traced back t
that ultimate foundation, law includes other principles whic
have been devised by men. Some of them can be shown t
be common to all nations. "The Roman people apply a la
which is partly its own, and partly is common to all men.'
Gaius's words are quoted in the *Institutes ;* both in th
Institutes and in the *Digest* his definition of *ius gentium* provide
the explanation of the cosmopolitan character of Roman law.

Finally, allowance had to be made for the solid core c
purely Roman institutions which had become the law of th
universal Empire. The *ius civile* derives its name from th
civitas. There have been many cities and many laws. Bu
"when we do not specify of what city we are speaking, we mea
our law"—the law of the Romans (*Inst.*, I, ii, 2).

There is little incoherence in all this. There is rather a
appraisal of the causes of the universal validity of Roma
law which closely corresponds to the facts. The trichotom
ius civile—ius gentium—ius naturale may have been a post
classical insertion. But it reflects, in a simplified form, wha
had actually been the different stages in the long process o
the universalization of Roman law, that process which, in Vico'
opinion, and in that of many great thinkers after him, represent
a sort of ideal pattern of all legal evolution.

The meaning and function of *ius gentium* have been describe many times. It was certainly the most important factor in that evolution. Under the stress of the growing intercourse with foreign peoples, the Roman jurists found in it the practical means for overcoming the limitations and extending the boundaries of municipal law ; until in due time it developed into a theoretical principle expressing the common element in all legislation. But the meaning and function of *ius naturale*, more subtle and less spectacular, requires some further assessment.

It is only by keeping in mind the practical use of such expressions as *ius naturale*, *naturalis*, *natura*, that we can hope to understand the part which was played by the corresponding notions in the heyday of Roman legal development. A careful survey of their manifold applications provides convincing evidence that they were invoked in the most different fields. They were invoked to provide a basis of rights and of duties. But that basis was not of a speculative, transcendental kind. It can best be described as a quest for the intrinsic character of a given situation.

Such words as *natura hominis*, *natura rei*, which recur so often in the texts, seem to indicate nothing more than the "normal" condition of men and of things. *Contra naturam* means the abnormal ; illness is described in one place as the "unnatural" condition of the body. The word *naturalis* indicates the condition of fact which is the presupposition of legal regulation. Thus there is a *naturalis possessio* at the root of all property. There is a *naturalis obligatio*, which may or may not be legally protected, but which is the necessary prerequisite of all obligations. There is a *cognatio naturalis* which must be distinguished from the *cognatio civilis*, in accordance with the two aspects, the "biological" and the political, of the Roman family.

Ius naturale played indeed a considerable part in Roman jurisprudence. But it had little to do with legal philosophy ; it was rather—as has been suggested—a "professional construction of lawyers" (Schulz). What the Roman jurists were striving after was to find the rule corresponding to the nature of things, to a concrete situation of fact and of life. In short, *ius naturale* was to them not a complete and ready-made system of rules, but a means of interpretation. Along with *ius gentium*, with which it was certainly connected and possibly for a time even identified, it played a decisive part in the process of adapting positive law to changing conditions and in elaborating the legal system of an international or rather super-national civilization.

Now it is impossible to believe that the Byzantine compilers should not have been aware of this particular, legal and not philosophical, meaning of the notions which were incorporated in the texts which they preserved, faithfully or not, for posterity. However anxious they may have been to stress the notion of natural law as a moral standard and to give prominence to it as the ultimate foundation of all laws and the expression of divine providence, there is one essential point in which they did not forgo what can well be called the most characteristic feature of the Roman conception of *ius naturale*. On this point that conception is as widely different from the medieval and modern, as it is from the essentially philosophical views which, under the influence of Stoicism, had been put forward by Cicero in the passage quoted at the beginning of this chapter. Here we reach possibly the very heart of the matter, where an explanation might be found of the difficulties in which so many students of that conception have become involved.

Nowhere, in fact, do we find in the *Corpus Iuris* an assertion of the superiority of natural to positive law, in the sense that in a case of conflict, the one should overrule the other. The Roman conception of natural law is anything but a revolutionary principle. It contains no vindication of the "rights of man". Neither has it much in common with the notion of a "higher law," such as is laid down in some modern constitutions. Being in itself merely "a reflection upon existing law," it was not meant to give "legal sanction to what was not otherwise law". In fact, it "was overruled in cases of conflict by what *was* law" (Zulueta). However contrary to natural law such institutions as slavery could still appear, even to the Byzantine lawyers, as perfectly justifiable and legal. We must indeed divest ourselves, in order to understand the Roman conception of natural law, not only of the modern conception of natural rights, but of the notion of the subordination of positive to natural law with which later ages have made us familiar. If this should be a disappointment to those who expected too much of the "perfectly continuous history" of natural law, let them not forget that the Roman doctrine had some other undeniable merits.

First and foremost is its lasting achievement in founding a system of law of unequalled completeness and harmony. The greatness of that achievement cannot be better described than in the following passage from Maine's *Ancient Law* :

> "I know no reason why the law of the Romans should be superior to the laws of the Hindoos, unless the theory of Natural Law had given it a type of excellence different from the usual one. In this one exceptional instance, simplicity and symmetry were kept before the eyes of a society whose influence on mankind was destined to be prodigious from other causes, as the characteristics of an ideal and absolutely perfect law."

These words offer a striking confirmation of what I suggested in the Introduction, viz., that the real significance of natural law must be sought in its function rather than in the doctrine itself. Because of that very function, the notion of natural law came to be as it were embodied in the Roman tradition, and was able to exert an influence which it would hardly have exerted had it remained in the regions of philosophical abstraction.

A system of law which purported to be grounded on its intrinsic value rather than on its power of compulsion was a unique experiment in the history of mankind. Roman legal tradition has taught the Western world to conceive of law as the common substance of mankind, as an unceasing effort to realize *quod semper aequum ac bonum est*. Let us read the Roman definitions with all necessary caution. *Semper* may have been an interpolation. Unlike the Byzantine Emperor, the classical Roman jurist may not have conceived of natural law as an immutable and eternal standard. There still remains the demand that law should correspond to nature, to equity and justice.

This demand has not been forgotten. In later days, historical circumstances and the very perfection of the Roman system of laws could lead to its veneration as the embodiment

B

of natural justice. It could be hailed as universally valid because of its coincidence with the law of nature. This belief was not the outcome of only medieval credulity. It was maintained down to more recent days. In a letter to Hobbes of July, 1670, Leibniz declared that, in his endeavour to reduce Roman law to its general elements, he had found that a clear half of it consisted of "pure natural law."

We may not share that belief any longer. But we cannot be entirely insensitive to the demand which the Roman jurists expressed. It is this demand, more than their actual definitions, which will always make the doctrine of natural law a subject of interest to the student.

GENERAL LITERATURE

R. W. and A. J. CARLYLE, *A History of Medieval Political Theory in the West*, Vol. I, 1903, P. 1 and 2.

The Legacy of Rome (Oxford, 1923) : *The Conception of the Empire*, by E. BARKER ; *The Science of Law*, by F. DE ZULUETA.

C. H. McILWAIN, *The Growth of Political Thought in the West*, 1932, Chapter iv.

H. F. JOLOWICZ, *Historical Introduction to the Study of Roman Law*, 1932.

F. SCHULZ, *Principles of Roman Law*, 1936; and *History of Roman Legal Science*, 1946.

SIR P. VINOGRADOFF, *Roman Law in Medieval Europe*, 2nd ed., 1929

The references to the *Institutes* and the *Digest* are from the Berlin edition (Krüger-Mommsen) of 1889 ; those to Cicero's *De Re Publica* and *De Legibus* from Loeb's Classical Library.

The survey of the references to *ius naturale, naturalis, natura*, is taken from an Italian work by C. A. MASCHI, *La concezione naturalistica del diritto e degli istituti giuridici romani*, 1937.

A useful selection of texts can be found in F. SENN, *De la justice et du droit*, 1927.

Historical and critical study of Roman Law has developed, in the last hundred years, and particularly in Germany and in Italy, into an immense literature which cannot be referred in detail. To the English reader the most inspiring approach to Roman Law and jurisprudence may perhaps still be provided by GIBBON's *Decline and Fall*, Chapter xliv.

CHAPTER II

A RATIONAL FOUNDATION OF ETHICS

"Mankind is ruled by two laws : Natural Law and Custom. Natural Law is that which is contained in the Scriptures and the Gospel." These words are taken from another great law-book, the authority of which for a time evenly balanced that of the *Corpus Iuris Civilis*. They form the opening paragraph of the *Decretum Gratiani* (ca. 1140), the oldest collectio of Church law embodied in the *Corpus Iuris Canonici*.[1] They provide the best introduction to the medieval conception of the law of nature.

Once again that ancient notion was called to play a capital role in the history of thought. In the hands of professional philosophers it became the corner-stone of a complete system of ethics. But that remarkable achievement would probably not have been possible had not the notion of natural law undergone a thorough transformation. The lawyers of the Church—the Canonists—stand out among medieval lawyers for the freedom and daring with which they recast the whole problem of law and morals. They gave natural law an unprecedented coherence, clearness and force. Canon law has been said, and correctly, to constitute the principal vehicle, in the Middle Ages, of the doctrine of the law of nature[2].

---

[1] *Corpus Iuris Canonici* was the name adopted by the Council of Basle in 1441 to indicate several collections of Church laws of which the first—the *Concordia discordantium Canonum*—is reminiscent of the *Digest*, the others of the *Code*. The *Concordia*, or as it is usually called the *Decretum Gratiani*, was the work of an Italian monk, Gratian, who was active in Bologna, the great medieval centre of law studies, in the first half of the twelfth century.

[2] This, according to Sir Frederick Pollock, is the explanation of the fact that the doctrine of natural law was never popular among English lawyers. *In Anglia minus curatur de iure naturali quam in aliqua regione de mundo*, wrote an early commentator of Bracton. For a further discussion of the relationship between the law of nature and the Common law, see Sir W. Holdsworth, *A History of English Law*, Vol. II, App. ii.

It is best to begin by reducing that doctrine to its simplest expression. Natural law goes back to God. Its precepts derive their authority from the fact that they are confirmed and implemented by Revelation. Properly speaking, natural law is essentially the concern of man. The old "legal tradition" —says an early commentator of Gratian referring to Ulpian's definition—defined natural law in the most general terms as that law "which nature has taught all animals". "But we shall disregard so general an acceptation and consider the meaning of it essentially in relation to matters which are proper to the human race alone."

Because of its divine character, natural law is absolutely binding and overrules all other laws. It precedes them in time, "because it came into existence with the very creation of man as a rational being, nor does it vary in time but remains unchangeable" (*Decr. Grat.*, P.I., dist. v, 1, § 1). It also precedes them in dignity. "Natural law absolutely prevails in dignity over customs and constitutions. Whatever has been recognized by usage, or laid down in writing, if it contradicts natural law, must be considered null and void" (*Decr. Grat.*, I, viii, 2). This statement of Gratian is still further reinforced by his commentator : "it must be considered null and void because the Lord has said *I am the Truth*, not *I am Custom or Constitution*".

These are strong and sweeping phrases. They make us aware that we have entered a very different world from that of the Roman lawyers. And yet it is not altogether impossible to trace the process by which the cautious and often ambiguous phrases of the Roman lawyers about natural law came to be modified and extended to provide a platform for the startling assertions of the medieval writers. As far as the "formal" continuity of the notion is concerned, there is no doubt that medieval natural law is the progeny of the Greeks and the Romans. To medieval eyes the idea of the law of nature appeared surrounded by the glamour of the Roman legal inheritance. It had, however, received as it were the necessary christening by being accepted and embedded in the teaching of the Christian Fathers. Scholars are still discussing to what extent the Christian notion of natural law is derived from Stoic philosophy or is a native product of Christianity.[1] However closely the Stoic and the Christian notions of the law of nature may resemble each other, there are undoubtedly subtle and far-reaching differences between them, derived from a different ideal and view of life.

There is, at any rate, nothing new nor staggering in Gratian's assertion of the divine and absolute character of the law of nature. That character had been emphatically asserted by Cicero ; and Lactantius, in preserving and quoting Cicero's famous definition of natural law, had pointed out that not even a Christian could have given a better one.   In the hands of the Fathers, natural law had come to be identified with the law given by God to Adam, the "general and primitive law of mankind".   Justinian, the Christian law-giver, had stressed in the *Institutes* the immutable character of the laws of nature, based on the providence of God.

Nor is there anything very surprising in the restriction of natural law to essentially human concerns, as against the general instinct of all animals and beings.   Cicero's *recta ratio in iubendo et vetando* as well as Gaius' *naturalis ratio* had laid the emphasis on the inherent capacity of man to discover the universal principles of law.   However different their conception of man, Christian writers like St. Ambrose or St. Augustine had developed the notion of a *lex naturalis in corde scripta* and of an *innata vis* to attain to the knowledge of it.   There could be little difficulty on the part of Christians in accepting a notion which seemed so pertinently to confirm the Apostle's saying of the Gentiles, "which shew the work of the Law written in their hearts, their conscience also bearing witness" (*Rom.*, II, 15).

Finally, not even the twofold division of law, which supersedes the tripartite division of the *Digest*, is entirely without precedents.   In laying it down at the beginning of his compilation, Gratian could refer to the authority of a Christian writer of the seventh century, whose encyclopaedic work— the *Etymologiae*—exerted a deep influence on medieval literature.   It is from St. Isidore of Seville that the sweeping generalization is taken : "All laws are either divine or human.

[1] For a full discussion of this problem, see the works of E. Troeltsch, to which I have called attention in a lengthy note to the Introduction.

Divine laws are based on nature, human laws on custom. The reason why these are at variance is that different nations adopt different laws."

Thus again it is perfectly possible to build up a strong case for the continuity of the natural law tradition which seems to leave little room for original thinking. But once again that continuity is misleading. The importance of Gratian's definition was not in what lay behind, but in what lay ahead of it. It is no exaggeration to say that in those simple words was contained the whole programme of medieval moral and legal philosophy. The words have a double meaning which must not be overlooked. They mean that the law of nature is embodied in the Scriptures. But they also mean that the Scriptures do not contradict the law of nature. The evidence of reason and that of Revelation are correlative. The Christian religion is no longer a "folly", a flat contradiction of human nature and the abolition of the old Adam. Worldly and godly wisdom must be reconciled. Reason and faith are not incompatible. Christianity can be implemented and enriched by philosophy.

The spirit of medieval Christianity can alone account for the part which natural law was called upon to play in this new conception of ethics. It is a different spirit from that of primitive Christianity. No doubt the Fathers of the Church had drunk deep at the well of heathen philosophy. They had not hesitated to accept whatever notions could be squared with Christian belief and used as a means of enhancing it. Natural law was one of the most prominent among them. Both St. Ambrose and St. Augustine could stress the natural capacity of man to attain to the knowledge of what is good and conducive to perfection. But at bottom the contrast between the world and the Kingdom of God remained a capital issue. In the manner of conceiving that contrast, however, there had been oscillations.

The extreme view is that which we still associate with Augustinianism. The fifth book of St. Augustine's *City of God* remains the most dramatic illustration of the dilemma which faced Christian ethics. In that book St. Augustine had discussed the virtues of the ancient Romans. They had been great and beneficent. The Romans had given the world free

institutions and good rulers. They had set the love of their
country above their own interest and welfare. Virgil is quoted
at length to provide evidence for the greatness of Rome.
It was thanks to their virtues that the Romans had achieved
"so many wonderful deeds, worthy of praise and of glory
according to the judgment of men". God had rewarded those
virtues by giving them "the worldly glory of the most excellent
Empire". But what were such virtues else than illusions?
What but smoke and vanity is the glory of the Earthly City
compared to the glory of the Heavenly? "What does it
matter to man, in this brief mortal life, under whose rule
he lives, provided the rulers do not force him to do evil?"
(*De Civitate Dei*, V, xvii). In such words all political interest
seems to have come to a standstill. One almost hears in them
the echo of a crumbling world. They mark the end of an epoch.

Not all Christian writers had gone to such extremes.
Social and political institutions could not fail to be a matter
of concern to the Christian. A rational explanation of their
existence and necessity could be given by welding together
the philosophic notion of a contrast between nature and
convention and the religious idea of human corruption and
sinfulness. Actually the belief in the corruption of human
nature could help to explain the hardships and miseries of
man's present conditions, while the idea of a divinely appointed
remedy could lead men to conceive of the State as an expression
of God's inscrutable providence. From such premises a body
of political philosophy could be elaborated which dominated the
West for many centuries. It is a philosophy of pessimism.
With nature corrupt, with an absolute ideal of Christian
perfection, little room was left for a natural order of things, for
a system of ethics based on man's nature. The function of
natural law was narrowly circumscribed. It was called in to
express a forsaken ideal, a condition of things irretrievably
lost to fallen humanity. It did not provide the rational basis
for social and political institutions.[1]

[1] Many modern historians, following Troeltsch, distinguish in the
teaching of the Fathers a " primary " or absolute, from a "secondary" or
relative, natural law, the first corresponding to nature before the Fall, the
second to the corruption of man's sinful nature. But these expressions are
nowhere to be found in the sources.

It is this rational basis which natural law was asked to provide by medieval thinkers. The old pessimism has gone. If anything, the Middle Ages seem to have been over-optimistic. The City of God is no longer an unattainable ideal. It is in this world that man is called to achieve it. The rigid alternative which had been stressed by St. Augustine has given way to an entirely new view of man's perfectibility. Christianity has ceased to be hostile to the world; it tends to be reconciled with it in a thoroughly Christian civilization. Such a staggering change would hardly have been possible had not new and powerful factors been at work in producing it. The medieval world was fluid, with avenues open to the future. Nothing had yet taken the place of the old bureaucratic structure of the Empire. The work of building up a Christian community could be started from below rather than from above.

An immense task lay ahead of the medieval man. The present had to be secured, the past reconquered. The lesson of Roman law was that the greatest of all legal systems had been based purely on reason and utility; the lesson of Aristotle, that the State is the highest achievement of man and the necessary instrument of human perfection. How could a Christian community be taught the elementary duties of good life and fellowship? How could Roman law be accepted as the universal law of Christendom? How could the teaching of Aristotle, the pagan philosopher, be adapted to the Christian view of life? If so great a body of wisdom had been discovered without supernatural help, if a basis was to be provided for human relations independently of the higher requirements of Christian perfection, surely there must be a knowledge of ethical values which man can attain with the sole help of his reason. There must be a system of natural ethics. Its corner-stone must be natural law.

This entirely new function for the idea of the law of nature is nowhere more apparent than in the teaching of St. Thomas Aquinas. He is the greatest representative of medieval philosophy as well as the most constructive and systematic thinker of the Middle Ages. His great *Summae* contain the most complete statement of that ideal of a thorough Christianization of life which inspired medieval Catholicism and which found its highest artistic achievement in the *Divine Comedy* of Dante. Although Thomist philosophy was at first bitterly opposed by contemporary schools of thought, it finally won the battle. It has remained ever since the most authoritative expression of what may well be called the Catholic view of life. We can therefore safely choose St. Thomas's theory of natural law as the best illustration of the part which that notion was called upon to play in one of the great constructive periods of Western civilization.

It is, however, impossible to understand that theory correctly without taking a resolute plunge into the vast sea of metaphysics. Before becoming a practical principle which, as we shall presently see, is susceptible of the most various applications, St. Thomas's theory of natural law is laid down as an interpretation of man's nature and of his relation to God and to the universe. Natural law is unintelligible unless we realize its close link with the eternal divine order on which the whole creation ultimately rests.

"Supposing the world to be governed by divine Providence . . . it is clear that the whole community of the universe is governed by the divine reason. This rational guidance of created things on the part of God . . . we can call the Eternal law.

"[Now] since all things which are subject to divine Providence are measured and regulated by the Eternal law . . . it is clear that all things participate to some degree in the Eternal law, in so far as they derive from it certain inclinations to those actions and aims which are proper to them.

"But, of all others, rational creatures are subject to divine Providence in a very special way; being themselves made participators in Providence itself, in that they control their own actions and the actions of others. So they have a certain share in the divine reason itself, deriving therefrom a natural inclination to such actions and ends as are fitting. This participation in the Eternal law by rational creatures is called the Natural law. Thus when the Psalmist said (*Psalm* IV, 6): 'Offer up the sacrifice of justice,' he added, as though being asked the question, what is the sacrifice of justice, ' Many say, who sheweth us good things ? ', and then replied, saying : 'The light of Thy countenance, O Lord, is signed upon us.' As though the light of natural reason, by which we discern good from evil, and which

is the Natural law, were nothing else than the impression of the
divine light in us.   So it is clear that the Natural law is nothing
else than the participation of the Eternal law in rational creatures"
(*Summa Theologica*, 1a 2ae, quae. 91, art. 1 and 2).

I have given St. Thomas's definition in full.   I shall now
try to disentangle the different points which seem to me to call
for attention in this context.   The first is the conception of
natural law as the expression of the dignity and power of man.

Alone among created beings, man is called to participate
intellectually and actively in the rational order of the universe.
He is called to do so because of his rational nature.   Reason is
the essence of man, the divine spark which makes for his
greatness.   It is the "light of natural reason" which enables us
to "discern good from evil".   St. Thomas's notion of the light
of reason is of capital importance.   It probably goes back to
Platonic and Augustinian sources, and has remained also in
later days closely associated with the notion of the law of nature.
It has been suggested that St. Thomas rationalized the illumina-
tion doctrine which St. Augustine had derived from Plato.[1]
He certainly used that doctrine in a humanist rather than in a
mystical sense.   The dignity and power of man lead up to an
interpretation of life which has been very aptly described as
a "Christian humanism".   Man is conceived to hold the unique
position of being at the same time a subject of God and His
co-operator, a position which Dante—a good Thomist on this
point—compared to the horizon "which lies in the middle,
between two hemispheres" (*Monarchia*, III, xvi).   Man par-
ticipates in two worlds ; hence the law of his nature includes
the qualities which he has in common with all created beings
as well as those which are distinctive of his own rational nature.

In a very interesting passage St. Thomas described how
the first and general precept of natural law—"do good and
avoid evil"—can be specified in a concrete order of precepts.
Man has in common with all created things the desire for self-
preservation.   Hence a first group of natural law precepts comprises all that makes for the preservation of human life.   But man
also has in common with animated beings a further inclination

---

[1] I owe this suggestion to Fr. F. C. Coplestone, S.J., in a private letter.

to more specific ends. Hence it is right to say that "that which nature has taught all animals" pertains to the natural law— such as sexual relationships, the rearing of offspring and the like. But, finally, "there is in man a certain inclination to know the truth about God and to live in society. In this respect there come under the Natural law all actions connected with such inclinations" (*Summa Theol.*, 1a 2a, 94, 2). St. Thomas was a great systematizer. In his classification the definition of Ulpian has found its proper place. But so have the reservations which medieval writers had felt it necessary to make in regard to it. Natural law, the expression of reason, cannot fail to be an essentially human concern.

The second point which calls for attention is the manner in which natural law is conceived as providing the basis of morality. This is a direct consequence of the dignity and power attributed to human nature. The central idea is here a particular notion of the relationship between the evidence of nature and that of Revelation. In giving a clear formulation to this idea, St. Thomas was fulfilling, as it were, what had been the deepest and most intimate aspiration of medieval Christianity. His assertion that "Grace does not abolish Nature but perfects it" is nothing but the translation into metaphysical terms of the attitude which I have already analyzed and described. It is the crown of that "Christian humanism" which is the essence of his philosophy.

The celebrated formula expresses not only an entirely new interpretation of the relationship between reason and faith, between philosophy and Christianity. It also contains a new and different notion of the capacities of human nature and of the effect of sin upon it. The idea of sin and its consequences could not but remain for St. Thomas a fundamental dogma of the Christian faith. But, as he expressly puts it, sin itself has not invalidated "the essential principles of nature". Its consequences concern only the possibility of man's fulfilling the dictates of "natural reason", not his capacity to acquire knowledge of them. In other words, they do not impair the existence of a sphere of purely natural— i.e., rational—values. It is in this sphere that the foundation of social and political institutions must be assessed.

Thus the possibility was opened up of giving a rational explanation and justification of ethical imperatives, as well as of all those institutions which earlier Christian thinkers had conceived as the result of sin and as its divine remedy. It was a momentous discovery, for it made it possible to accept the Aristotelian conception of ethics and politics and to graft it, as it were, on the Christian interpretation of life. This is not the place to examine the historical significance of the Aristotelian revival and its manifold consequences in the field of social and political theory.[1] But it is important to remark that it would not have been possible for St. Thomas to accept and revive Aristotle's theory of the State had his notion of natural law not provided the necessary instrument. A positive value could be attributed to the State as the highest expression of natural morality. Man could be conceived as a political animal, finding in the life of the community the harmonious integration of his individual life. The contrast between nature and convention, though never openly rejected, ceased for a time to play any prominent part in political theory.

Yet natural law was not only the foundation of morality and of all social and political institutions. It was also the paramount standard by which these institutions could be judged. This is the third point which must be kept in mind in order to understand the doctrine correctly. In this point also St. Thomas brings out clearly and logically what had been in the minds of his contemporaries. The Christian community must be based on justice. And justice, as disclosed to man in the precepts of natural law, must prevail over any other command or authority. "Whatever has been recognized by usage, or laid down in writing, if it contradicts natural law must be considered null and void." The words of the Canonist are faithfully re-echoed by St. Thomas—and an adequate explanation is provided.

"St. Augustine says : 'There is no law unless it be just.' So the validity of law depends upon its justice. But in human affairs a thing is said to be just when it accords aright with the

[1] For further information I venture to refer the reader to my book on *The Medieval Contribution to Political Thought* and to my Introduction to AQUINAS, *Selected Political Writings*, 1948.

rule of reason : and, as we have already seen, the first rule of reason is the Natural law. Thus all humanly enacted laws are in accord with reason to the extent that they derive from the Natural law. And if a human law is at variance in any particular with the Natural law, it is no longer legal, but rather a corruption of law" (*Summa Theol.*, 1a 2ae, 95, 2).

This is no academic statement devoid of any practical significance. The words must be taken literally. They mean that allegiance to the State—even though it be the highest embodiment of natural morality—can be only conditional. Unjust laws are not properly laws. "They do not, in consequence, oblige in conscience."

> "Man is bound to obey secular rulers to the extent that the order of justice requires. For this reason if such rulers have no just title to power, but have usurped it, or if they command things to be done which are unjust, their subjects are not obliged to obey them, except perhaps in certain special cases, when it is a matter of avoiding scandal or some particular danger " (*Summa Theol.*, 2a 2ae, 104, 6).

Thus, in certain cases, disobedience may not only be a possibility, but a duty. A theory of resistance can be built up on such premises. The final decision, however, is a matter of complex casuistry. It does not rest solely with the individual. We must be careful not to misconstrue the medieval theory of resistance into a theory of revolution.

In fact, despite the stress which is laid upon the absolute and immutable character of natural law, the notion of it seems to be curiously flexible and adaptable. Positive laws are not expected to be moulded upon it as upon a rigid pattern. A considerable sphere of freedom is left to the human law-giver in the interpretation and application of its general precepts. St. Thomas indeed goes so far as to admit that natural law can change. It can change by "addition", as when new institutions become necessary in view of the development of human activities. It can change by "subtraction", when "something ceases to pertain to the Natural law which was formerly part of it". It is thus quite clear that natural law can be superseded on grounds of utility. In certain cases it seems to indicate simply a condition of things which would prevail if, in the interest of human life, human reason had not been led to adopt new devices. Thus it is possible to speak of a "common possession of all things", and of an "equal liberty of all men". Neither private property nor slavery were imposed by nature. Natural law was not altered but simply added to by their adoption (*Summa Theol.*, 1a 2ae, 94, 5).

This seems to bring us back to the pragmatism of the Roman lawyers. But it is the attitude to history which calls for attention. We tend to consider the very notion of natural law as a typical form of unhistorical thinking. The assertion of absolute and immutable values seems to imply the denial of evolution and development. A correct appraisal of St. Thomas's notion of natural law may lead us to modify these conclusions. However different it may be from our own, a deep feeling for history pervades his legal philosophy. The largest possible allowance is made for historical circumstances, the largest compatible with belief in truth and in justice. History is not the last resort, nor can it provide man with the ultimate standard. "The Lord has said *I am the Truth*, not *I am Custom or Constitution*."

Lastly, we must consider the limitations of natural law. They considerably qualify the significance of the whole theory. The law of nature is not the only law which guides man on his way to perfection. Other laws are necessary. Human laws must be established to draw out all the conclusions of natural law, and "to restrain evil men from wrongdoing by force and by fear". Divine laws were revealed in order to lead man to his heavenly destination, to remedy the weakness of human judgment, to probe the secrets of man's heart and thus to leave no evil unforbidden and unpunished. All law, eternal and natural, human and divine, is linked together in a complete and coherent system. As Hooker remarked—and Hooker was probably one of the ablest, and certainly one of the most unbiased defenders of Thomist legal philosophy—"as the actions of men are of sundry distinct kinds, so the laws thereof must accordingly be distinguished . . . If we measure not each by his own proper law, whereas the things themselves are so different, there will be in our understanding and judgment of them confusion" (*Ecclesiastical Polity*, II, i, 2).

But in order fully to appreciate the inherent limitations of natural law we must never forget that, in the Thomist conception, the natural order is only the condition and the means for the attainment of a higher order. If "Grace does not abolish Nature", neither does nature abolish grace.   Reason and faith go hand in hand, but reason is the handmaid.   In the end it is faith alone which can lead man to his "end of eternal blessedness".   The gradual progress of the soul towards God is symbolized in Dante's long and perilous voyage.   The words which the poet attributes to Virgil can well be applied to St. Thomas's notion of natural law :

> ". . . So far as reason plead
> Can I instruct thee ; beyond that point, wait
> For Beatrice ; for faith is here thy need."
> (*Purgatorio*, xviii, 46-48.   Binyon's transl.)

And in the same way as Virgil hands over his pupil to Beatrice on the summit of the mountain of Purgatory, so does the law of nature constitute for man only a step, although a necessary step, towards perfection.

This is the essential qualification of the Thomist conception of natural law, and we must always keep it in mind lest we entirely misconstrue St. Thomas's endeavour to base a natural system of ethics on it.   Natural law is the token of the fundamental harmony between human and Christian values, the expression of the perfectibility of man and of the power and dignity of his reason.   But the system of ethics which is based on these assumptions cannot properly be called a "rationalist" system.   The proud spirit of modern rationalism is lacking. There is no assertion of man's self-sufficiency and inherent perfection.   There is no vindication of abstract "rights", nor of the autonomy of the individual as the ultimate source of all laws and of all standards.

No doubt a system such as this can be said to contain a recognition, and indeed a defence, of human personality.   It can be developed, as has been done by some modern Thomists,[1] into a codified system of human rights based on the Christian

[1] J. MARITAIN, *The Rights of Man and Natural Law* (1944).

view of the supreme value of the individual soul, the goal of Redemption. But on closer inspection it is only too evident that the "rights of the human person" of the Thomist are something entirely different from the "rights of man" which will be examined in the following chapter. The assertion of those rights is always based on the existence of an objective standard of justice. The emphasis is on natural law, not on natural rights. What is stressed is the duty of the State rather than the rights of the individual, the restoration of the right order of things rather than the perilous experiment of revolution. In fact, it is not from the individual that we are asked to start, but from the Cosmos, from the notion of a world well ordered and graded, of which natural law is the expression.

The modern Thomist will insist that the proper foundation of natural law is a metaphysical foundation. But the metaphysics which he has in mind is the Christian, or rather the Thomist. His starting point is that of St. Thomas: "supposing the world to be governed by divine Providence". The theorists of natural rights also had their metaphysics. They also had their providence. But it was no longer the Thomist, perhaps it was not even the Christian providence.

Thus once again the real significance of the notion of natural law seems to lie more in its function than in the doctrine itself. The stroke of genius of medieval writers was to have grasped its importance for the foundation of a natural system of ethics, distinct though not separate from Christian or revealed ethics. Natural law was the instrument for solving a problem which, from the Christian standpoint, might otherwise seem insoluble or non-existent. Augustinianism and Thomism are often said to constitute the two correlative though not necessarily contradictory poles, so to speak, of Christian thought. The Thomist interpretation of Christianity is unthinkable without the notion of natural law.

That notion has remained a lasting inheritance of legal and moral philosophy. Its importance, one might say, transcends the setting of circumstance and time which explain it historically. It represents a fundamental attitude of the Christian towards the problem of life and society. It has outlived St. Thomas as well as medieval Catholicism. The

Protestant Hooker made full use of it against the intransigent Augustinianism of the Puritans. It is more than a paradox that this notion should have provided the basis for a defence of the Church of England and indeed of what would nowadays be called the English way of life. The best appreciation of the medieval notion of natural law can be given in Hooker's own words : "these School-implements are acknowledged by grave and wise men not unprofitable to have been invented".

GENERAL LITERATURE

R. W. and A. J. CARLYLE, *A History of Medieval Political Theory in the West*, Vols. II-V.

O. von GIERKE, transl. by MAITLAND, *Political Theories of the Middle Ages*, 1900/1922.

J. N. FIGGIS, *Political Aspects of St. Augustine's "City of God,"* 1921.

B. JARRETT, *Social Theories of the Middle Ages*, 1926.

C. H. MCILWAIN, *The Growth of Political Thought in the West*, Chapters v-vi.

SIR M. POWICKE, *The Christian Life in the Middle Ages*, 1935.

E. GILSON, *The Spirit of Medieval Philosophy*, 1936.

A. P. D'ENTRÈVES, *The Medieval Contribution to Political Thought*, 1939.

French books: O. LOTTIN, *Le droit naturel chez Saint Thomas d'Aquin et ses prédécesseurs*, 1931 ; H. X. ARQUILLÈRE, *L'Augustinisme politique*, 1934.

German : O. SCHILLING, *Naturrecht und Staat nach der Lehre der alten Kirche*, 1914, and *Die Staats- und Soziallehre des hl. Thomas von Aquin*, 1923 ; E. BERNHEIM, *Mittelalterliche Zeitanschauungen in ihrem Einfluss auf Politik und Geschichtsschreibung*, 1918.

The references to the *Decretum Gratiani* are from the Leipzig edition (Friedberg) of 1879 ; those to St. Thomas Aquinas from my edition of *Selected Political Writings*, 1948.

For the attitude of the Canonists to natural law, W. ULLMANN, *Medieval Papalism*, 1948, should now be consulted. I regret that I was unable to make use of it as the present essay was already with the printer at the time of its publication.

A THEORY OF NATURAL RIGHTS

"The Representatives of the French people, constituted in a National Assembly, considering that ignorance, oblivion or contempt of the Rights of Man are the only causes of public misfortunes and of the corruption of governments, have resolved to lay down, in a solemn Declaration, the natural, inalienable and sacred Rights of Man, in order that this Declaration, being always before all the members of the Social Body, should constantly remind them of their Rights and their Duties ; that the actions of the Legislative as well as of the Executive Power being liable at any moment to be referred to the end of all political institutions, should be more respected ; that the grievances of the citizen, being henceforward based upon simple and indisputable principles, should always be conducive to the preservation of the Constitution and to the happiness of all."

THESE solemn words form the preamble of the *Déclaration des Droits de l'Homme et du Citoyen.* Together with the fall of the Bastille, the Declaration adopted by the French National Assembly on the 26th of August, 1789, opened the way to the French Revolution. The proclamation of the "natural inalienable and sacred rights of man" marks the end of an era and the beginning of contemporary Europe.[1] How tempting it is to consider it only the final act in two thousand years of uninterrupted development ! According to many historians the theory of the rights of man had "been implicit in political thought ever since the Stoics and as a result of Rome's transmission of Stoic conceptions of equality" (McIlwain). I have in the preceding chapters raised some doubts as to the continuity of that development. They will be further confirmed if we submit the modern theory of natural rights to the same critical examination to which the Roman and the medieval notions of natural law have been subjected.

[1] See note at the end of this chapter.

Once again it seems best to begin by considering the outstanding features of the theory. They can be reduced to three. The first is its rationalism. The "natural rights of man" are conceived to be equivalent to "simple and indisputable principles". The second, its individualism. The talk is about the "natural, inalienable rights of *man*" ; and men, it is said, in the first of the seventeen articles contained in the Declaration, "are born and remain free and equal in rights". The third outstanding feature of the theory is its radicalism. The exercise of power is "liable at any moment to be referred to the end of all political institutions" ; and the end of all political institutions, we read in Article 3, "is the preservation of the natural and imprescriptible rights of man". Even more forcibly, the American *Declaration of Independence* had asserted, thirteen years earlier, that "whenever any form of government becomes destructive of these ends, it is the Right of the People to alter or abolish it".

The rationalism of the theory first calls for attention. There had always been a rationalist bent in the notion of the law of nature. It had been closely associated with the working of "natural reason". It had been identified with the dignity and power of man. But reason to the Roman lawyer was perhaps only another name for experience. For the medieval philosopher it was the gift of God. In both cases the evidence of reason had to be implemented, and indeed confirmed, by some other evidence—of fact or of faith. But now the evidence of reason is in itself sufficient. "We hold these truths to be self-evident," wrote the American Fathers. The French re-echoed the idea of the existence of "simple and indisputable principles" as the ultimate standard and the basis of political obligation.

Rationalism is an ambiguous word. It would take a long time to define it. It would take still more to trace its subtle ramifications and the infinite varieties of its manifestations. "The appearance of a new intellectual character is like the appearance of a new architectural style ; it emerges almost imperceptibly, under the pressure of a great variety of influences . . . All that can be discerned are the slowly mediated changes, the shuffling and reshuffling, the flow and ebb of tides of inspiration which issues finally in a shape identifiably new." This remark by a recent student of "rationalism in politics"[1] fully applies to the modern theory of natural law. Both in the American and in the French Declaration the rationalist style is easily identifiable, and startling enough. But it is not so easy to trace its origin and to ascertain the moment in which it shows itself unmistakably for the first time. The emphasis laid on the continuity of the natural law tradition has led, in this as in other instances which we have examined, to some misconstructions which must be carefully assessed.

Hugo Grotius, a Dutchman (1583-1645), has long been considered the founder of the modern theory of natural law. This judgment goes back to Pufendorf (1632-1694), the first holder of a chair of Natural Law in a German university, and the greatest academic expounder of the theory in the seventeenth century. Pufendorf praised Grotius as the *vir incomparabilis* who dared to go beyond what had been taught in the Schools, and to draw the theory of the law of nature out of the "darkness" in which it had lain for centuries. That judgment is still repeated in many handbooks. Along with Bacon and Descartes in the field of philosophy, with Galileo and Newton in the field of experimental science, Grotius has a special place reserved in the field of jurisprudence as one of the prophets of our brave new world.

This view has been challenged by some modern historians. They have gleefully set to work revising the accepted version and displacing Grotius from his pedestal. There is nothing new nor original—so the story is now told—in the notion of natural law which Grotius used as the foundation of his treatment of the *Laws of War and Peace* (1625). The tradition of natural law had continued to flourish in Europe all through the sixteenth century, notwithstanding the fact that the unity of Christendom had been torn asunder by the Reformation of which Grotius was a son. That notion had been accepted by Catholic as well as by Protestant writers. Grotius did nothing but borrow it from the late Scholastics, particularly from the Spanish theologians and legal philosophers to whom he

[1] M. OAKESHOTT, *Rationalism in Politics*, in " The Cambridge Journal," Vol. I, 1947.

acknowledged his indebtedness. His thought, therefore, is "a direct continuation of the great Natural Law tradition which stretches from St. Augustine to Suarez, and which culminated in St. Thomas."[1] His famous dictum that natural law would retain its validity even if God did not exist (*etiamsi daremus non esse Deum*), can be traced back to earlier writers. It is far less revolutionary than it seems, and it is actually accompanied by very important cautions and qualifications.

Once again the quest for precedents has led historians to forget that a doctrine must not be judged by the letter, but by the spirit. There is no doubt that all the great thinkers who open up our modern age have their roots in the age that preceded them. But the fact that Descartes—as has been conclusively shown—drank deep at the well of Scholastic philosophy is certainly no reason for mistaking him for a Schoolman. Nor is the possibility of tracing a large literature *On the Government of Princes* in the Middle Ages an excuse for overlooking the startling novelty of Machiavelli's *Prince*. If Grotius—like Machiavelli and Descartes, and many other great thinkers—was considered by his contemporaries and his immediate successors to have broken with the thought that preceded him, we must try to understand the reasons which led to that opinion. These reasons are not difficult to ascertain. They throw light upon the emergence of that "rationalist" notion of natural law which found its complete expression one and a half centuries later.

It is not in its content that Grotius' theory of natural law breaks away from Scholasticism. It is in its method (Cassirer). His definition of natural law has nothing revolutionary. When he maintains that natural law is that body of rules which man is able to discover by the use of his reason, he does nothing but restate the Scholastic notion of a rational foundation of ethics. Indeed, his aim is rather to restore that notion which had been shaken by the extreme Augustinianism of certain Protestant currents of thought. When he declares that those rules are valid in themselves, independently of the fact that God willed them, he repeats an assertion which had already been made by

[1] A.-H. CHROUST, *Hugo Grotius and the Scholastic Natural Law Tradition*, in "The New Scholasticism," Vol. XVII, 1943.

some of the Schoolmen for reasons which will be discussed in the following chapter.[1] He is careful to put forward that view in such a way as to avoid any suggestion of blasphemy.

> "What we have been saying would have a degree of validity even if we should concede that which cannot be conceded without the utmost wickedness, that there is no God, or that the affairs of men are of no concern to Him" (*De Iure Belli ac Pacis*, Prolegomena, § 11).

This is a purely hypothetical argument. It is quite clear that Grotius, still deeply imbued with the spirit of Christianity, would never have conceded that God did not take any part in the affairs of men. The law of nature is implanted in man by God. It has therefore unquestionably a divine origin (*ibid.* § 12). The revealed laws of God confirm and assist men in their knowledge of the law of nature (§ 13).

But Grotius' aim was to construct a system of laws which would carry conviction in an age in which theological controversy was gradually losing the power to do so. He therefore proceeded on the hypothesis further than anyone had done before him—much further than even the judicious Hooker, whose inclinations and thought bear so close a resemblance to his. He proved that it was possible to build up a theory of laws independent of theological presuppositions. His successors completed the task. The natural law which they elaborated was entirely "secular". They sharply divided what the Schoolmen had taken great pains to reconcile.

The doctrine of natural law which is set forth in the great treatises of the seventeenth and eighteenth centuries—from Pufendorf's *De Iure Naturae et Gentium* (1672) to Burlamaqui's *Principes du Droit Naturel* (1747), and Vattel's *Droit des Gens ou Principes de la Loi Naturelle* (1758)—has nothing to do with theology. It is a purely rational construction, though it does not refuse to pay homage to some remote notion of God. But, as C. Becker remarked, God is increasingly withdrawn from immediate contact with men. The laws of nature are to Jefferson the Laws of Nature's God. The French legislators solemnly put themselves "in the presence and under the

[1] See below, Chapter IV, page 71.

auspices of the Supreme Being". But Nature's God or the Supreme Being are not more akin to the God Omnipotent of the Creed than Deism is to Christianity. What Grotius had set forth as a hypothesis has become a thesis. The self-evidence of natural law has made the existence of God perfectly superfluous.

Here we touch on another point in which Grotius' influence was decisive. If natural law consists in a set of rules which are absolutely valid, its treatment must be based upon an internal coherence and necessity. In order to be a science, law must not depend on experience, but on definitions, not on facts, but on logical deductions. Hence, only the principles of the law of nature can properly constitute a science. Such a science must be constructed by leaving aside all that undergoes change and varies from place to place.

> "I have made it my concern to refer the proofs of things touching the law of nature to certain fundamental conceptions which are beyond question ; so that no one can deny them without doing violence to himself. For the principles of that law, if only you pay strict heed to them, are in themselves manifest and clear, almost as evident as are those things which we perceive by the external senses" (*De Iure Belli ac Pacis*, Prolegomena, § 39).

The analogy with mathematics is at hand. It provides the best illustration that natural law cannot be altered even by God.

> "Measureless as is the power of God, nevertheless it can be said that there are certain things over which that power does not extend . . . Just as even God cannot cause that two times two should not make four, so He cannot cause that that which is intrinsically evil be not evil" (*De Iure Belli ac Pacis*, I, i, x).

It provides the new methodological assumption which Grotius prides himself on having introduced into the study of law.

> "With all truthfulness I aver that, just as the mathematicians treat their figures as abstracted from bodies, so in treating law I have withdrawn my mind from every particular fact " (*Ibid.*, Prolegomena, § 58).

Grotius claimed for his treatment of legal problems the merit of clarity, self-evidence and coherence. These qualities were fully appreciated by his successors.

Nowhere is the "rationalist" character of the new conception more apparent than here. The analogy between mathematics and justice had precedents which went back to Plato. It was fully developed by Pufendorf and Leibniz, and survived even in Montesquieu. It was destined, however, to decline in the eighteenth century under the impact of empirical and utilitarian thought. But the idea that the theory of law should be based on clarity, self-evidence and coherence, remained the dominating mark of legal philosophy down to the revolutionary era.

Rationalism indeed is here the very synonym of anti-historicism. The evidence of history cannot shake the absolute validity of natural law. Its only interest is to provide an object for further generalisations, or illustrations of the "ignorance" and "darkness" which has long befallen humanity and which reason must dispel. Vico, a lonely voice, pleaded in vain for a different conception. For him, the "ideal, eternal law" could be fully revealed only in the long ordeal and suffering of mankind. But for the rationalist thinker the self-evident law of nature was in want of no confirmation. It could make history if necessary. It actually did so in the end.

Rationalism, however, is not the only distinctive character of the modern conception of natural law. Its impact upon thoughts and events would not have been so great if it had only expressed a particular manner of thinking. It was an assertion of values as well. The new value is that of the individual. Individualism is the second outstanding feature of modern natural law. The word is not less ambiguous than rationalism. There had been a Greek individualism as well as a Roman. There is a Christian individualism which has deeply pervaded our religious interpretation of life. The quest after "origins" would again lead us far back, perhaps to Protagoras' dictum that man is the measure of all things.

But when we read the American or the French Declarations we know that we are confronted with a complete architecture, about the style of which there can be no mistake. It is a political philosophy based upon a particular notion of the individual, of society and of their mutual relationship. What Jefferson called the "station" to which nations and men are entitled under "the laws of Nature and of Nature's God" has become the determining factor in political obligation. It is a pattern of ideas for which it is difficult to find precedents in history, and it has left an indelible mark upon our civilization.

As with the emergence of rationalism, it is impossible to determine with absolute certainty the moment when modern individualism was born. The part played by the Renaissance and the Reformation in shaping the new conception of man has often been analysed and described. We all agree, I suppose, that it is at some time in the beginning of the modern era that we must locate the rise of that individualistic principle which held several generations under its spell, until it finally found the way to a sweeping transformation of the whole social and political structure of the Western hemisphere. There is, however, one moment from which we can date the introduction and the coherent application of the individualistic principle in political philosophy. It is the moment at which political theorists turned to the idea of contract for their interpretation of the relationship between the individual and the community. It is the moment when the doctrine of the social contract first makes its appearance.

I am speaking, of course, of the social contract proper, the notion of an agreement between individuals as the origin of civil society. Political theory has known other uses of the contractual idea, such as the contract of government or the contract of submission. This is a theory which "has nothing to do with the origin of society itself, but, presupposing a society already formed, purports to define the terms on which that society is to be governed" (Gough). This theory had medieval roots, and it played an important part in the religious and civil dissensions which mark the beginning of modern Europe. It lingered on even in later days, and it is sometimes not easy to distinguish it from the social contract proper. But the theory of the social contract, apart from occasional precedents which can be found in ancient writers, is an entirely modern product. It is the distinctive mark of the political theory of individualism. It is closely associated with the modern theory of natural law.

Indeed, the theory of the social contract would hardly have been possible had not the modern notion of natural law provided its basis. There was nothing new in the assertion that man is a rational being, capable of guiding himself and of deriving from his reason a standard to judge his environment. There was nothing new in the notion that man is born free and equal to all other men ; in the idea of an original state of nature ; in the quest for an explanation of the change which had come about with the rise of social and political institutions. It is only a shifting of accent on these commonplaces of natural law theory which can explain why all of a sudden we are faced with a doctrine which purposely sets out to construe civil society as the result of a deliberate act of will on the part of its components.

The shifting of accent is the same which we have analysed in the transformation of natural law into a purely rational and secular principle. The accent is now on the individual. The social contract was the only possible way left for deducing the existence of social and political institutions once the reason of man was made the ultimate standard of values. The construction bears the unmistakable mark of rationalist thinking. It provided what Mr. Oakeshott would call a political "crib" : in his recent article on *Rationalism in Politics*, Mr. Oakeshott has convincingly shown that one of the main concerns of rationalist thought was to provide such cribs in all fields of learning.

The social contract was a crib. It was also a blue-print. Its different interpretations have all one character in common. Their starting point is the individual. Their basis is the modern, secular notion of natural law and the "station" of man which is derived from it. This is true even of the contract which gives rise to the "great Leviathan," to Hobbes' "mortal God". Hobbes' political theory is the extreme outcome of rationalism and individualism—as it were the *reductio ad absurdum* of both. The different interpretations of the contract and of its consequences are merely the result of different interpretations of human nature, that is, of the impact of natural law upon man.

Man may be throughout a reasonable creature, or he may

be dominated by lust or fear. Accordingly, the manner of conceiving the "station" of man will vary, as well as the interpretation of what Cicero had already called the *causa coëundi*, the reason for men joining together in society. But if we take the most widely different authors—say Hobbes and Locke—we cannot fail to be aware of the fact that the essential elements —the form and the substance—of the contract remain unvaried in all. "Formally," the contract is a manifestation of individual will with the object of establishing a relationship of mutual obligation which would not otherwise exist by the law of nature. "Substantially", the content of the contract is the "natural right" of the individual, which is exchanged against a counterpart of equal or greater value—the benefits of society and the security of political organization. The social contract may effect a complete transformation of the original right, as is the case with Hobbes and Rousseau. Or it may leave that right unaltered, and have no other purpose than to secure it, as Locke was anxious to maintain. But in all cases the contract is the necessary pattern of all legal and political obligations.

How did it come about—Maitland asked—that political theory borrowed from the lawyers the notion of contract, "that greediest of legal categories", and made it the basis of the State ? The answer can only be given in the words of Kant, who reaped the fruit of the age-long development. The idea of contract was the only possible means of setting the natural rights of the individual within the framework of the State.[1] The theory of the social contract may have been to begin with a theory of the origins of political society. It was also and primarily a rational explanation of the State, the only explanation compatible with the pattern of thought laid down in the modern notion of natural law.

But the mention of "natural rights" brings us back to the *Déclaration* and to the third outstanding feature of modern natural law. Radicalism is a less ambiguous word than individualism or rationalism. The modern theory of natural law was a rational construction. It was an assertion of the value of the individual. But it was also and foremost a

[1] KANT, *Rechtslehre*, §47.

vindication of rights. As such, it could become a theory of revolution. It had become one by 1776 and 1789. Curiously enough, there was nothing revolutionary in modern natural law in its beginnings. Jefferson's radical assertion, that any form of government which proves destructive of the "inalienable rights" of man should be altered or abolished, is more reminiscent of the uncompromising statements of medieval lawyers and philosophers than of the abstract speculation of the earlier theorists of modern natural law.

Medieval political theory had elaborated a doctrine of resistance to "unjust" or "unlawful" government. That doctrine lived on through the Renaissance, the Reformation and the Counter-Reformation. It was given prominence and actuality in the great social and political upheavals of the sixteenth century. It was fully developed by that group of writers who, for their advocacy of the right of rebellion, came to be named *Monarchomachi* (literally the enemies of kings). That group includes Protestant as well as Catholic authors. It is interesting to note that, as recent historians have pointed out, Protestant writers seem to be inclined to justify the right of resistance on grounds of history or of scripture rather than of natural law. The tendency towards rational and "natural law" arguments is more prominent among the Catholic *Monarchomachi*.

However that may be, the school of natural law of which Grotius is considered the founder had little to do with either group. On the Continent, that school flourished under the benign rule of the absolute princes, when the problem of resistance was no longer an issue and new interests were focussed on legal and political thought. In England, both the Puritan and the Glorious Revolutions had centred on practical issues rather than on abstract speculations. Ever since Burke, the contrast between the assertion of the "rights of Englishmen" and the vindication of the "rights of man" has become a commonplace in the interpretation of English history.

The question then is, how did it come about that the doctrine of natural law, which Grotius had lifted up to the highest regions of abstraction, and which had from the start assumed the character of a scientific rather than a practical principle, became a revolutionary doctrine which changed the face of the world ? This is a large question which would involve the discussion of the several factors which contributed to the unprecedented development of thought during the century and a half that divides the appearance of *The Laws of War and Peace* from the first shot fired at Concord by the "embattled farmers" whose guns were "heard round the world". But there is one point which throws light on the process as it were from within : a point which ought to have been kept in mind from the beginning and which must now be squarely faced and assessed.

The modern theory of natural law was not, properly speaking, a theory of law at all. It was a theory of rights. A momentous change has taken place under cover of the same verbal expressions. The *ius naturale* of the modern political philosopher is no longer the *lex naturalis* of the medieval moralist nor the *ius naturale* of the Roman lawyer. These different conceptions have in common only the name. The Latin word *ius* is the cause of the ambiguity. It has its equivalent in most European languages, except in English.[1] The fact is significant. As Hobbes pointed out with his usual shrewdness :

> "though they that speak of this subject use to confound *ius* and *lex*, *right* and *law :* yet they ought to be distinguished ; because RIGHT consisteth in liberty to do, or to forbear : whereas LAW determineth, and bindeth to one of them : so that law and right differ as much, as obligation and liberty" (*Leviathan*, P. 1, Chapter 14).

The different meanings of the word *ius* had of course long been familiar to the lawyers who had been brought up in the study of the Roman law. They had carefully distinguished between "objective" and "subjective right", between the *norma agendi* (the rule of action) and the *facultas agendi* (the right to act) which can both be indicated by the same name of *ius*, and which are indicated in English by the different names of law and of right. But they had never overlooked the fact, which

[1] For a detailed analysis of the different meanings of *law*, *right* and *ius* see Sir J. SALMOND, *Jurisprudence* (Eighth ed., 1930), Appendix I.

Hobbes seems either to ignore or implicitly to deny, that the two meanings of *ius* are not antithetic, but correlative. In the language of the law-schools, *ius* could be used in an "objective" as well as in a "subjective" sense : but the latter always presupposes the former. There is a *facultas agendi* in as much as there is a *norma agendi*. There is a "right" in as much as there is a law.

The distinction is capital if we are to understand the full implications of the modern theory of natural law. The great majority of natural law writers in the seventeenth and eighteenth centuries would not have accepted Hobbes' anarchical conception of "natural right" as opposed to "natural law".[1] To them natural law was the necessary presupposition of natural right. Locke, in his *Second Treatise of Government* (Chapter vi, § 59 and 63) makes the point very clearly. He says that the natural freedom of man is nothing else than his knowledge of the law of nature, in the same way as the freedom of an Englishman consists in his "liberty to dispose of his actions and possessions" according to the laws of England. But the emphasis is shifting more and more from the objective to the subjective meaning of natural law. Wolff, towards the middle of the eighteenth century, declares quite flatly that the latter is the only proper meaning of *ius naturae* and that

> "whenever we speak of natural law (*ius naturae*), we never intend the law of nature, but rather the right which belongs to man on the strength of that law, that is naturally" (*Ius Naturae Methodo Scientifica Pertractatum*, 1741, tom. I, Prol., § 3).

On the eve of the American and French Revolutions the theory of natural law had been turned into a theory of natural rights. The old notion which lawyers, philosophers and political writers had used down the ages had become—to use Professor Willey's expression—a liberating principle, ready to hand for the use of modern man in his challenge to existing institutions. Even then, the two meanings survived. The doctrine of natural rights was closely associated with that of a "fundamental law", the American version of the Con-

---

[1] The opposite view is taken by L. STRAUSS, *The Political Philosophy of Hobbes*, 1936, page 156.

tinental idea of the law of nature. The *Declarations of Rights,* of which the Virginia Bill opened the series, clearly expressed the belief that a solemn document was necessary to provide "the basis and foundation of government".

But it was the vindication of the rights of man which gave modern natural law its tremendous power and vigour. Rationalism, individualism and radicalism combined to give the old word an entirely new meaning. The notion which had been invoked to construct a universal system of law and to provide a rational foundation for ethics, inspired the formulation of a theory of rights which will not easily be cancelled from the heart of Western man and which bears witness to his generosity and idealism.

NOTE.—I long hesitated whether to choose as the heading of this chapter the opening words of the American *Declaration of Independence* or the preamble of the French *Declaration of the Rights of Man.* I finally decided for the French declaration, though I am fully aware of the soundness of Sir Ernest Barker's remark that "we who live in Europe too readily see the year 1789 as the year in which it was said: 'Behold, I will make all things new.' A wider view will show us that the year of change was the year 1776 . . ."

The connection between the two Declarations, or, as the word now goes, between the two ideologies, the American and the French, is still a matter of controversy. It has produced, and not only in English, a large literature which this is not the place to discuss. Perhaps the best illustration of that connection is provided by two documents existing in the Library of Congress in Washington to which O. Vossler first called attention. They are two original drafts of the *Déclaration des Droits de l'Homme* submitted by Lafayette to Jefferson, American ambassador in Paris till September 1789, for discussion and criticism: one of them bears Jefferson's autograph remarks.

Here, at any rate, are the opening paragraphs of the American *Declaration* of 1776, to which many references will have been found in the text of this chapter:

"When in the Course of human events, it becomes necessary for one people to dissolve the political bands, which have connected them with another, and to assume among the powers of the earth, the separate and equal station to which the Laws of Nature and of Nature's God entitle them, a decent respect to the opinions of mankind requires that they should declare the causes which impel them to the separation. We hold these truths to be self-evident, that all men are created equal, that they are endowed by their Creator with certain unalienable Rights, that among these are Life, Liberty and the pursuit of Happiness. That to secure these rights, Governments are instituted among Men, deriving their just powers from the consent of the governed. That whenever any form of Government becomes destructive of these ends, it is the Right of the People to alter or to abolish it, and to institute new Government, laying its foundation on such principles and organizing its powers in such form, as to them shall seem most likely to effect their Safety and Happiness."

GENERAL LITERATURE

C. E. VAUGHAN, *Studies in the History of Political Philosophy before and after Rousseau*, 1925.

C. BECKER, *The Declaration of Independence*, 1922 ; and *The Heavenly City of the Eighteenth Century Philosophers*, 1932.

B. F. WRIGHT, *American Interpretations of Natural Law*, 1930.

C. G. HAINES, *The revival of Natural Law Concepts*, 1930.

H. J. LASKI, *The Rise of European Liberalism*, 1936.

I. W. GOUGH, *The Social Contract*, 1936.

B. WILLEY, *The Eighteenth Century Background*, 1940.

C. J. FRIEDRICH, *Inevitable Peace*, 1948.

SIR E. BARKER, *Natural Law and the American Revolution*, in *Traditions of Civility*, 1948.

D. J. BOORSTIN, *The Lost World of Thomas Jefferson*, 1948.

German books : O. von GIERKE, *Johannes Althusius und die Entwicklung der naturrechtlichen Staatstheorien*, 1880/1913 (English transl. by B. Freyd, *The Development of Political Theory*, 1939) ; W. DILTHEY, *Weltanschauung und Analyse des Menschen seit Renaissance und Reformation (Gesammelte Schriften*, II) ; G. JELLINEK, *Die Erklärung der Menschen- und Bürgerrechte*, 4th ed., 1927 ; O. VOSSLER, *Die Amerikanischen Revolutionsideale in ihrem Verhältnis zu den Europäischen*, 1929, and *Studien zur Erklärung der Menschenrechte*, 1930 ; E. CASSIRER, *Die Philosophie der Aufklärung*, 1932 ; (English transl. by F. C. A. Koelln and J. P. Pettegrove, *The Philosophy of Enlightenment*, 1951).

French and Italian: B. FAY, *L'esprit revolutionnaire en France et aux Etats Unis à la fin du XVIIIe siecle*, 1924 ; B. GROETHUYSEN, *Origines de l'esprit bourgeois en France*, I, *L'Eglise et la Bourgeoisie*, 1927 ; P. HAZARD, *La crise de la conscience européenne*, 1680-1715 (1932) ; D. MORNET, *Les origines intellectuelles de la Révolution Française*, 1715-1787 (1947) ; G. DEL VECCHIO, *Su la teoria del contratto sociale*, 1906.

The references to GROTIUS, *De Iure Belli ac Pacis Libri Tres*, are from F. W. Kelsey's translation (*The Classics of International Law*, Publication of the Carnegie Endowment for International Peace, No. 3, 1925).

C

CHAPTER IV

THE ESSENCE OF LAW

ANOTHER and different approach to our subject can now b
suggested. Enough evidence has been provided of th
historical function of natural law. The time has come t
assess its general value. That value, if any, can consist onl
in a specific contribution to the knowledge of law and to th
understanding of legal phenomena.

The doctrine of natural law was closely associated wit
historical development. But some of its features are constan
The theorists of natural law were faced with much the sam
problems as confront the modern legal philosopher. Th
first of these problems is that of the essence of law. It is
problem of form or of structure. It is a problem of definitio
"Is law an act of the will or of the intellect ?" Is the existenc
of a superior and an inferior the necessary pattern of leg
experience ? The question may be put in these or in othe
terms, but it is still controversial. The old discussion abou
the nature of *ius*—whether *ius quia iustum* or *ius quia iussum*[1]—
was more than an etymological quibble.

Natural law provided a definite answer. It stands or fal
with a particular notion of law. The very condition of it
existence is that the identification of law and command b
overcome or abandoned. Its logical outcome is an extension o
the concept of law which is much more far-reaching an
exacting than is at first realized. This is nowhere more apparer
than in the many challenges which natural law had to mee
in its age-long development. We must begin by examinin
these challenges. The grouping which is adopted in thi
chapter should not be taken to imply a chronological successio
It is rather a description of types or modes of thought whic
have recurred at different epochs. We are here concerne
only with what they have in common.

[1] This is a play upon words, *iustum* meaning "just," and *iussu*
"commanded."

The most direct and obvious challenge comes from the
legal field proper. It is the challenge of what in our days is
called legal positivism. It is the challenge of a particular
experience in which command and obedience appear as the
essential attributes of law. But the Austinian definition of law
is no present-day novelty. It has more than one precedent
in the past. There were legal positivists long before Austin.
There is an understandable bias towards positivism in all
lawyers. Here is a quotation from Cicero which may serve
to remind us how old the issue is :

> " ATTICUS : Then you do not think that the science of law
> is to be derived from the Prætor's edict, as the majority do now,
> or from the Twelve Tables, as people used to think, but from
> the deepest mysteries of philosophy ?

> "MARCUS : Quite right ; for in our present conversation,
> Pomponius, we are not trying to learn how to protect ourselves
> legally, or how to answer clients' questions. Such problems
> may be important, and in fact they are . . . But in our present
> investigation we intend to cover the whole range of universal
> Justice and Law in such a way that our own civil law, as it is
> called, will be confined to a small and narrow corner " (*De
> Legibus*, I, v, 17).

Clearly Cicero's idea is that the essence of law cannot be fully
understood unless we go beyond the "popular view" that law
is simply a command or a prohibition (*ib.*, I, vi, 19). Positive
law is unable to tell us the last word about the real nature of
legal experience. "The civil law of the Roman people" should
be "confined to a small and narrow corner".

Actually Roman law became the law of the civilized world.
It provided the mainstay of Europe's legal education for
centuries to come. And the notion of law which was embodied
in the Roman texts was the outcome not so much of philosophical speculations as of a particular historical experience.
Law was to the Romans the object of a deliberate act of legislation. Law was the expression of the will of the Roman
people, or of the Emperor to whom the original power of the
people had been transferred. It was left for later generations
endlessly to discuss the nature of that transference, and to

derive from the Roman texts conflicting evidence in favour o
monarchy or of democracy.

But the real importance of those texts lay in the notic
they contained, that all law must go back to an ultimate powe
which expresses and sanctions it. The holder of that powe
is the source of the law. He is therefore above the law—
legibus solutus. The Byzantine prince, as he emerges from th
pages of Justinian's law-books, is the living embodiment of th
law—*lex animata*, νόμος ἔμψυχος. He is such, not in th
sense in which Aristotle had conceived the excellent king t
be a living law because of his exceptional personal qualities, bu
in a strictly legal sense, because of his office of law-give
because of the attribute of sovereignty which is inherent i
legislation. Thus, in the Roman tradition, sovereignty and la
became correlative notions.

Sovereignty of course is a comparatively modern expression
Bodin, a French sixteenth century writer, claimed to be i
inventor.[1] But, as he himself admitted and his contemporarie
were quick to point out, the notion went back to a tradition o
thought which had already borne its fruits in the Middle Age
Long before the theorists of the State, the theorists of th
Church had resorted to the notion of a *potestas legibus solut*
to make good the claim of the medieval Papacy to world domina
tion. And in turn the idea of a supreme and ultimate powe
from which all laws proceed went back to the Roman tex
that the Bolognese lawyers had rediscovered in the elevent
century. From them a new and revolutionary notion of la
was revealed to medieval Europe.

The importance of the doctrine of sovereignty can hardl
be overrated. It was a formidable tool in the hands of lawyer
and politicians, and a decisive factor in the making of moder
Europe. It was also an object of passionate controvers
It met with enthusiastic support and with unbending resistanc
from different quarters and in different countries. But it als
appeared to undermine the very possibility of natural la
thinking. Natural law is not properly law if sovereignty
the essential condition of legal experience. It is not possib

---

[1] JEAN BODIN, *De la République*, 1576.

conceive a law of nature if command is the essence of law. How then can it be explained that the notion of natural law survived, and indeed blossomed into new life, even after the doctrine of sovereignty had been finally accepted as the necessary presupposition of the modern State ?

The answer to this question provides a further qualification of Figgis' famous dictum about the *damnosa hereditas* of Roman law. For Roman law was no doubt the vehicle of the doctrine of sovereignty. But it was also one of the vehicles of natural law, which it fostered with all its glamour and authority. And a correct reading of the Roman texts certainly provided the means for circumscribing the notion of sovereignty within precise and well-defined limits. These limits were those of positive law. The notion of sovereignty was—at least in origin—a strictly legal, not a philosophical notion. Unless we bear this in mind we shall be unable properly to understand the peculiar contribution of Roman ideas to political theory.

Sovereignty was not to the Romans a synonym of lawlessness. On the contrary, in a famous passage of the *Corpus Iuris Civilis*, the Emperor is described as deriving his power from the law and as being subject to its authority (*Codex*, I, 14, 4 : Const. "Digna Vox"). This is no contradiction to the notion of sovereignty. The fact that positive law is laid down in the form of a command and proceeds from the will of the sovereign does not mean that the holder of sovereignty is immune from all legal obligation. The point is set out with a wealth of imagery by medieval theorists of sovereignty. "The Pope—writes one of them—is an animal without reins and without bridle, the man who is above the positive law. Yet he must impose on himself reins and bridle, and live according to the established laws and observe them, unless special cases arise and particular causes require him [to alter them]."[1]

Clearly, the notion of sovereignty does not cancel the notion of legal obligation. Positive law does not exhaust the whole range of legal experience. There may be laws other than the commands of the sovereign, laws with a different structure yet nevertheless binding and formally perfect. The laws of

[1] AEGIDIUS ROMANUS, *De Ecclesiastica Potestate*, 1302 (ed. Scholz, 1929) lb. III, cap. 8.

the international community can look to no ultimate power fo
their enforcement. Natural law is devoid of sanctions. Yet bot
are properly called laws and are binding even on the sovereig
In the words of Albericus Gentilis—the Italian jurist, wh
taught Roman law at Oxford from 1587 to 1608—the "absolute
Prince is a prince who is *above* positive law but *under* natur
law and the law of nations.[1]

This doctrine was a product of the Roman law-school
of the Continent. In England it was unpopular and alien
But it provided the programme of legal and political thinkin
for the next two centuries. Never did the ideas of natural an
of international law flourish so happily and undisturbed as i
the age of princely "absolutism". This is a clear indicatio
that the challenge of legal positivism could be successfull
met if the nature of sovereignty were correctly appraised, an
the definition of law as a command were not taken as the fina
answer to the problem of legal experience.

The trouble is that the "voluntarist" notion of law was no
always limited to the legal sphere proper. A different challeng
to natural law could take shape the moment that notion wa
extended to all moral imperatives. Philosophers and theo
logians were more formidable foes than the professional lawyer
Mention must now be made of a much more insidious menac
to the doctrine of natural law, the Nominalist theory of ethics

Nominalism meant not only a crisis in Scholastic method
a quarrel about "universals" and an anticipation of som
aspects of the modern theory of knowledge. It also meant
radical change in the approach to morality. The vindicatio
of the primacy of the will over the intellect led to the denia
that ethical values can have any other foundation but th
will of God that imposes them. The notion of God as a
unlimited and arbitrary power implied the reduction of al
moral laws to inscrutable manifestations of divine omnipotence
The basis of the "natural system of ethics" was discarded

[1] ALBERICUS GENTILIS, *Regales Disputationes Tres*, 1605 (Disp. I, D
Potestate Regia Absoluta, p. 17). He in turn refers to Baldus, the medieva
jurist, as his source for the distinction. A. Gentilis is better known as th
author of the *De Iure Belli* (1598) and as one of the founders of moder
international law.

Natural law ceases to be the bridge between God and man. It affords no indication of the existence of an eternal and immutable order. It no longer constitutes the measure of man's dignity and of his capacity to participate in that order, a standard of good and evil available to all rational creatures.

This is how a recent historian describes the impact of Nominalism on ethics : "An action is not good because of its suitableness to the essential nature of man—but because God so wills. God's will could also have willed and decreed the precise opposite, which would then possess the same binding force as that which is now valid—which indeed, has validity only as long as God's absolute will so determines. Law is will, pure will without any foundation in reality, without foundation in the essential nature of things" (Rommen). It is as if the notion of sovereignty were here applied to the divine law-giver himself. The consequences were soon apparent.

Nominalism is, of course, used here only as a general name for a vast movement of thought and opinion. It may be doubted whether all the implications of "voluntarist ethics" are already traceable in Duns Scotus (1266-1308). But certainly they are fully drawn out by William of Ockham (1300-1350). And the notion of the moral law as the expression of the divine will passed over from the Nominalists to the Reformers —to Wycliff, and later on to Luther and Calvin.

The "sovereignty of God" is the pivot of Calvin's theology and ethics. The similarity between Calvin's notion of God as *legibus solutus* and the modern conception of sovereignty is a fascinating subject for research and reflection. The analogy has been pointed out many times, and attention has been called to Calvin's early training in the law as a possible source of his notion of God's sovereignty. In turn, it has been maintained that this notion could not fail to affect legal and political theory, and that many fundamental concepts of modern political theory are nothing but "secularised" theological concepts. Both views have some element of truth, though it would certainly be unwise to overrate it.

Protestantism did not necessarily lead to a complete break with the old tradition of natural law. The impact of the Reformation upon the continuity of legal and political thought is still the subject of controversy among scholars. But it seems obvious enough that the Thomist conception of natural law, as a mediatory element between God and man, and as an assertion of the power and dignity of human nature, would have been out of place in the Reformers' theology, and actually they found little or no room for it.

The Reformation marked a return to the rigid alternatives which had been stressed by St. Augustine and have been analysed in one of the preceding chapters.[1] It brought about a profound transformation of moral and political standards, which in turn could not fail to leave traces and to exert an influence upon the new conception of natural law which was the product of the Age of Reason. But, as far as the controversial literature of the period is concerned, the evidence, as has already been pointed out[2], is that the continuity of natural law thinking is more apparent among Catholic than among Protestant writers. The voluntarist bent of Protestant ethics may well afford an explanation of the comparative disparagement, among Protestant controversialists and political writers, of natural law in favour of the divine law of the Bible on one hand, and, on the other, of the positive law of the State conceived as ultimately grounded upon the will of God. That the "divine right of kings" is a typical product of this age is certainly significant.

One point, at any rate, is certain : that the revival of natural law which takes place towards the turn of the sixteenth and seventeenth centuries is essentially a rejection of the "Nominalist" or "voluntarist" theory of law. This is apparent in Hooker. It is equally apparent, and historically far more important, in Grotius. For Hooker was mainly restating the old Thomist arguments against his Puritan opponents. But Grotius was the founder of the modern theory of natural law.

Thus Grotius' famous proposition, that natural law would retain its validity even if God did not exist, once again appears as a turning point in the history of thought. It was the answer to the challenge of voluntarist ethics. It meant the assertion that command is not the essence of law.

[1] Above, pp. 36-37.
[2] Above, p. 58.

This, I think, is what must be kept in mind in order correctly to appraise the "precedents" of Grotius' much quoted dictum. The daring assertion that natural law is independent of the will of God had already been made by the Schoolmen, though not by Thomas Aquinas himself. The Spanish Jesuit Suarez, in his treatise *On the Laws*,[1] which Grotius quotes with great respect, gives a convenient summary of Catholic authors on the subject. There were indeed many, Suarez pointed out, who had taken the view that natural law, as an indication of what is "intrinsically good or intrinsically bad", does not depend on the will "of any superior".

> "These authors seem therefore logically to admit that natural law does not proceed from God as a law-giver, for it is not dependent on God's will, nor does God manifest Himself in it as a sovereign (*superior*) commanding or forbidding."

Indeed, some of these authors had gone so far as to say that

> "even though God did not exist, or did not make use of His reason, or did not judge rightly of things, if there is in man such a dictate of right reason to guide him, it would have had the same nature of law as it now has."

This, very likely, was the source of Grotius' statement about the validity and character of natural law. He was using an old argument, but the challenge which he endeavoured to meet was not an entirely new one either. The Nominalist doctrine that the will of God is the ultimate source of morality had played a prominent part in Protestant theology and ethics. Grotius was a Protestant, but, as a follower of Arminius, he rejected the extreme Calvinist view of the absolute sovereignty of God. But he was also a jurist, and his vindication of natural law was further devised to meet the new and dangerous challenge of the absolute sovereignty of the State. Grotius' capital importance lies in the fact that he succeeded where others had failed. He secured a new lease of life for the doctrine of natural law and for the notion that law is not merely an expression of will.

There was, however, a third possible line of attack on

[1] Franciscus Suarez, *De Legibus ac Deo Legislatore*, 1619, lib. II, Cap. vi.
C*

natural law which proved more devastating than the challenge of either legal positivism or voluntarist ethics. It was indeed more than a challenge. It was a complete reversal of positions. The notion of law as the expression of will could be met on purely legal grounds by restricting its validity to positive law and denying its application to other groups or types of legal experience. It could be met on the philosophical or theological plane by proving its inadequacy to explain the nature of God and of moral imperatives. But it is difficult with any of these arguments to meet a theory which as it were turns upside down the very pattern of natural law thinking. It is impossible to reconcile the notion of natural law with the doctrine of the "ethical state". This doctrine is usually associated with the name of Hegel.

The association is correct. For it is with Hegel that the final break with natural law occurs in legal as well as in political theory. Already in one of his earlier works—an essay on *The Scientific Treatment of Natural Law* (1802)—Hegel had called into question the whole tradition of thought which had centred on natural law.[1] Its theorists, he pointed out, had either contented themselves with generalisations from existing institutions which they were anxious to justify, or else been inspired by a purely "negative" attitude to ethics, thus exasperating a dualism between the ideal and the real which they had been unable to bridge. Hegel pleaded for a "positive" approach to the problem. The real task of ethics, he maintained, is to understand and assert the "totality" of ethical life. "The absolute ethical totality is nothing but *ein Volk*—a people or nation."

The momentous implications of this entirely new approach to law and morality were developed by Hegel in his *Philosophy of Right* some twenty years later (1821). The full title of the book is *Natural Law and Political Science in Outline*.[2] But there is no trace in it of natural law in any of its traditional meanings. *Recht* or *ius* Hegel defines in the most extensive

---

[1] G. W. F. HEGEL, *Über die Wissenschaftlichen Behandlungsarten des Naturrechts*, in *Hegels Schriften zur Politik und Rechtsphilosophie, Sämtliche Werke*, Vol. VII, ed. Lasson, 1913.

[2] The references are to T. M. Knox's translation, Oxford, 1942.

ense as the realization of "free" or "ethical" will. It therefore comprises all possible manifestations of moral life. Positive or civil law is but one of its aspects. Of ethical life the national State is the highest embodiment. Its "right" therefore stands above any other. The State is the ethical whole, the incarnation of God in history. Its basis "is the power of reason actualising itself as will". The rational will is the presupposition of all law and morality.

Hegel's theory of the "rational will" goes indeed far beyond the old quarrel whether reason or will constitutes the essence of legal experience. The doctrine of the ethical State is a complete substitute for the doctrine of natural law which had accompanied Western thought throughout its long history. It entirely reverses the relationship between the ideal and the real, which was the necessary presupposition of natural law thinking. The claims of natural law are to Hegel the outcome of the antagonism "between what ought to be and what is". It is an ineradicable bent of the human mind to contrast them. But true philosophy must overcome this antagonism. It must reconcile man to the historical world, which is his own creation. "The great thing is to apprehend in the show of the temporal and transient the substance which is immanent and the eternal which is present" (*Philosophy of Right*, Preface and Addition 1).

It is no easy task to appraise Hegel's teaching correctly. His famous dictum, "What is rational is actual and what is actual is rational," certainly allows of a twofold interpretation. It does not necessarily imply, as is often assumed, a plea for conservatism, a glorification of existing institutions as such. In one place, indeed, Hegel openly states that "in considering the Idea of the State, we must not have our eyes on particular States or on particular institutions. We must consider the Idea, this actual God, by itself" (*ibid.*, Addition 152).

Ideals can have a greater actuality than facts. Hegel's conception of the interplay of the ideal and the real could easily be turned into the most explosive theory of revolution. Marxism was an offspring of Hegelianism. But there can be no doubt that Hegel's conception of history marks the end of natural law thinking altogether. It eliminates for all purposes that notion

of an ideal law which, as we shall presently see, is anothe
constant feature of the theory of the law of nature. Ideal
cease to be immutable and eternal. They are the outcome o
history. It is before the bench of history that ideals must b
tried.

History had indeed been the stumbling block of all natura
law theories. Lawyers, philosophers and theologians had trie
in vain to account for the apparent indifference of historica
development to any pattern of right or wrong. Political theorist
of the past had found it difficult to square the bitter fact
of political life with the requirements of justice. Afte
Machiavelli had brought the crude contradictions betwee
morals and politics into the limelight, the convenient doctrin
of *raison d'état* had been invented to explain, if not to justif
the encroachments of political necessity on the field of accepte
morality.

But now that history was transfigured into the unfolding
of the Absolute, now that the State was conceived as the embodi
ment of ethical life, the exigencies of *raison d'état* could appea
in a different perspective. The opposition between moral
and politics could be declared to be the result of "superficia
ideas about morality," and the welfare of the State to hav
claims to recognition "totally different from those of the welfar
of the individual". Not the abstract precepts of natural law—
"the many universal thoughts supposed to be universal com
mands"—but the "concrete existence" of the State shoul
dictate its behaviour. It may happen that a higher moralit
is revealed "in the form of hussars with shining sabres", an
the vain harangues of the moralist will be silenced by th
"solemn cycles of history". Against the apparent injustice o
the State there is no appeal but to history, for "the history o
the World is the World's court of judgment" (*Philosophy o
Right*, §§ 337, 340 ; Addition 188).

I have no intention of dwelling at greater length on th
niceties of Hegel's political theory. It would certainly b
unfair to attribute to the German philosopher the sole responsi
bility for later developments of thought which have born
such bitter fruit not only in his own country but also for th
whole of Europe. Actually the notion that will can be creativ

f ethical values is not strictly speaking an invention of Hegel's. Hegel himself acknowledged his debt to Rousseau. Rousseau's theory of the "general will" is the real source of the theory of the ethical state.

It is difficult to say how clearly Rousseau was conscious of breaking with the notion of natural law. "Rousseau is a Janus-like figure in the history of natural law. He turns to it, and belongs to it : he turns away from it, and belongs elsewhere" (Barker). But Rousseau is responsible for the doctrine that "whoever refuses to obey the General Will shall be compelled to do so by the whole body"—for "this means nothing else than that he will be forced to be free". And we have only to look at Rousseau's way of solving the problems which had been the crux of natural law thinking to realize the complete change which has come over legal and political theory :

> "On this view, we at once see that it can no longer be asked whose business it is to make laws, since they are acts of the General Will ; nor whether a prince is above the law, since he is a member of the State; nor whether the law can be unjust, since no one is unjust to himself ; nor how we can be both free and subject to the laws, since they are but registers of our wills." (*Du Contrat Social*, 1762, Book II, Chapter VI, trans. by G. D. H. Cole).

There can be little room left for old-fashioned discussions about the nature of justice and the essence of law when human will is made the supreme arbiter of all human values. Speaking of precedents, we may well note here that Rousseau had a striking and untimely forerunner in a medieval writer. Marsilius of Padua, a fourteenth century Italian, had stated in so many words a theory of the general will in his *Defensor Pacis* (1324). According to him, not only are laws the expression of the will of the people, but it is because they are the expression of the will of the people that laws are good and just. Natural law had never reigned quite unchallenged, not even in the Middle Ages.

Compared to Hegel, Rousseau or Marsilius, the author of *Leviathan* (1651) seems almost a moderate thinker. For all his insistence on sovereignty, for all his denial that natural law can properly be called a law, for all his assertion that it is positive law that lays down the "distinction of Right and

Wrong", Hobbes is nearer to the positions of voluntarist ethics than to those of the ethical state. His conception of law is the Nominalist conception. His ethical theory rejects the notion of absolute values. His State is an artificial, not an historical product. In the definition of the "mortal God" it is the adjective that matters. The "great Leviathan" still lacks the soul with which Rousseau and Hegel endowed it.

Let us bring matters to a head and attempt a conclusion. So far, only the negative side of the question has been examined. But it is the positive side that matters. In order to meet the challenge to natural law its supporters seem to have constantly fallen back upon certain fundamental premises. I submit that these premises are the necessary conditions of natural law thinking. Natural law was a definition of law. It implies an extension of the notion of law which may well perplex the modern student. I know of no better illustration of this point than the one which is given by Hooker. That "learned and judicious divine" had a real gift for bringing out, in an age of passionate controversy, the gist of an argument. This is what he wrote in the first book of his great treatise on *The Laws of Ecclesiastical Polity* (1594):

> "They who are thus accustomed to speak apply the name of *Law* unto that only rule of working which superior authority imposeth; whereas we, somewhat more enlarging the sense thereof, term any kind of rule or canon, whereby actions are framed, a law" (*Eccles. Polity*, I, iii, 1).

"Somewhat more enlarging the sense thereof": the words bear the mark of Hooker's well-known caution and balance. But they bring out the essentials. Hooker's title to greatness is that, more than any other writer, he can claim to stand between two ages and to constitute a link, if there is any, between the old and the new schools of natural law. I think that both the medieval and the modern theorists of natural law, however divergent their views might have been on other matters, would have agreed on the necessity of "enlarging the sense" of law which Hooker stresses.

Hooker's definition of law as "any kind of rule or canon whereby actions are framed" is almost word for word the definition of Thomas Aquinas. "Law"—St. Thomas maintained—"is a rule or measure of action in virtue of which one is led to perform certain actions and restrained from the performance of others" (*Summa Theol.*, 1a 2ae, 90, 1). Even friendly critics had been reluctant to follow St. Thomas so far. "Such a description," wrote Suarez, "seems to be too broad and general" (*De legibus*, I, i, 1). It is curious to find an Anglican more faithful to St. Thomas than a Jesuit. But Hooker had perhaps the clearer grasp of the issue.

He was set on breaking the spell of the Nominalist God. He knew that the notion of sovereignty could be harnessed only on certain conditions. He was putting St. Thomas' words into good English vernacular : "the being of God is a kind of law to His working."[1] But he was also handing on to later generations the notion of a law-abiding God and of a well-ordered universe. "Of law there can be no less acknowledged, than that her seat is the bosom of God, her voice the harmony of the world" (*Eccl. Pol.*, I, xvi, 8). This is sound Thomist doctrine. But it has also a strangely eighteenth century ring :

> "The spacious firmament on high,
> With all the blue æthereal sky,
> And spangled heavens, a shining frame,
> Their great Original proclaim."

The extension of the notion of law is a pronouncement on its nature. Law does not necessarily require the existence of a superior and an inferior. Law does not only command. It does something else besides which is no less important. Actually natural law *teaches*, according to Locke ; according to Grotius it *indicates* a particular quality of actions. This opens up new perspectives to the understanding of legal phenomena. A law which lacks authoritative sanction may yet be law. *Pacta sunt servanda*, the ultimate basis of international law, is such a proposition.

In turn a rule may be laid down as a command and yet not be properly a law. We must learn to distinguish in law the "compelling" from the "directing" element. This had led

---

[1] *Ecclesiastical Polity*, I, ii, 2 ; cp. AQUINAS, *Summa Theologica*, 1a 2ae, 93, 4.

the Schoolmen to a complex casuistry. They had distinguished two aspects of law, the *vis coactiva* and the *vis directiva*. It is the *vis directiva*, the element of justice which is embodied in law, that ultimately matters. And Grotius, going back to the warning of Cicero, had made a similar point:

> "Those who have consecrated themselves to true justice should undertake to treat the parts of the natural and unchangeable philosophy of law, after having removed all that has its origin in the will of man" (*De Iure Belli ac Pacis*, Prol., § 31).

The emphasis is shifted from *ius quia iussum* to *ius quia iustum*, from the form of the law to its content. And the content of the law is an ethical value. The relation between law and morals is the crux of the whole theory.

But even the formal structure of law could not fail to be affected by such premises. If law is not merely a command, if it does not only proceed from the will, law is the outcome of reason. Natural law is a plea for reasonableness in action. But it is also an assertion that only inasmuch as action can be measured in terms of reason does it properly come under the heading of law. It is because law is an act of the intellect that its notion can be extended to "any kind of rule or canon, whereby actions are framed." We find this difficult to accept and perhaps even to understand. But let us try to forget for a moment our everyday experience of legal positivism. Let us set aside the ambiguities of the word "reason" and the widely different meanings with which it was used in turn by the theorists of natural law. What we find is a definite proposition about the essence of law.

Law is a standard, a model, a pattern from which the quality of a particular action, the relevance of certain situations and facts may be inferred. The primary function of law is not to command but to qualify; it is a logical as well as a practical proposition. The notion of law has much wider implications than the professional lawyer would have us believe. Legal valuations are possible where we are no longer accustomed to expect them. Legality is an aspect of moral experience which extends far beyond the legal field proper. I shall try to show in the concluding section of this book that such conceptions can still enrich our minds, and that the old discussions about the essence of law should not be wilfully ignored by the modern legal philosopher.

GENERAL LITERATURE

On the doctrine of sovereignty : LORD BRYCE, *The Nature of Sovereignty*, in *Studies in History and Jurisprudence*, Vol. II, 1901 ; C. N. S. WOOLF, *Bartolus of Sassoferrato*, 1913.

On voluntarist ethics and its impact on Protestantism : G. DE LAGARDE, *Recherches sur l'esprit politique de la Réforme*, 1926.

On the theory of *raison d'état* : F. MEINECKE, *Die Idee der Staatsräson in der neueren Gerschichte*, third ed., 1929.

On the theory of the ethical State : B. BOSANQUET, *The Philosophical Theory of the State*, 1925; L. T. HOBHOUSE, *The Metaphysical Theory of the State*, 1918.

For a summary of the discussions on the essence of law : JETHRO BROWN, *The Austinian Theory of Law*, 1912, Excursus E

CHAPTER V

LAW AND MORALS

THE relation between law and morals is the crux of all natural law theory. The theory not only requires an extension of the notion of law. It also implies a definite view about its compass. The problem is no longer one of form or of structure. It is a problem of content. The content of law is a moral one. Law is not only a measure of action. It is a pronouncement on its value. Law is an indication of what is good and evil. In turn, good and evil are the conditions of legal obligation.

The problem of the content of law is far from being ignored by present-day legal positivists. They frankly admit that every system of laws corresponds to a particular "ideology". They refer to the "sociological background" as a necessary part of legal experience. They recognize that law is not only a command, but also the embodiment of certain values. The difference lies in the manner of conceiving those values. Natural law theorists would never have admitted that law is merely the expression of the standards of a particular group or society. They believed in absolute values, and they conceived of law as a means to achieve them. "Law is the furtherance of what is good and equitable." "There is no law unless it be just." "The end of all political association is the preservation of the natural and imprescriptible rights of man." I have chosen my quotations at random. We are no longer concerned with what divided their authors. We are concerned with what they had in common.

The close association of morals and law is the distinguishing mark of natural law theory throughout its long history.[1] The very enunciation of natural law is a moral proposition. The first precept of natural law, says Thomas Aquinas, is "to do

[1] Maitland, it may be remembered, connected the doctrine of natural law with " the jural conception of morality" (*Collected Papers*, I, p. 23).

good and to avoid evil."[1] And Grotius declares that "the law of nature is a dictate of right reason which points out (*indicans*) that an act . . has in it a quality of moral baseness or moral necessity."[2] From this general proposition both the old and the new school of natural law set out to construct a complete and precise code of rules. The only difference is the greater caution of the earlier theorists in drawing out the consequences and applications of their first "self-evident" principle.

I have already given a sample of the Scholastic manner of handling the subject. Several groups or categories of precepts can be deduced from the first and general precept that good should be done and evil avoided. They correspond to "the order of our natural inclinations" : self-preservation, the preservation of the species, life in society. Practically all social and political institutions—marriage, property, civil authority, etc.—can be shown to be derived from these original "values", and thus to partake of a moral character.

In contrast with this elaborate process of deduction, which allows for variations according to time and circumstances, stands the modern and rationalist doctrine of natural law with its blunt assertion of a constant and necessary pattern of social and political relations. The natural and imprescriptible rights of man, according to the *Declaration* of 1789, "are liberty, property, security and resistance to oppression".

Medieval philosophers seem to have been anxious to couch their ideals in loose and general terms. It is difficult, though not impossible, to relate these ideals to a particular social background. The "bourgeois ideology" is much more clearly defined. It shows the unmistakable imprint of its age and of the social and political struggle which it reflected. Yet in both it is a "table of values" that provides the foundation of all legal order. In both the assumption is that the validity of law depends on the measure in which these values are embodied in it. Only good laws are laws. And for a law to be good, it must be based, in one way or another, upon natural

[1] Above, p. 40.
[2] *De Iure Belli ac Pacis*, I, 1, 10.

law. "If a human law is at variance with natural law it is no longer legal." "A society where the respect of rights is not assured has no constitution."

Shall we then conclude that one, and perhaps the most striking, of the characteristics of natural law theory is to weld together morals and law in such a way that it is no longer possible to distinguish them? This is a capital question which calls for careful elucidation. The confusion between law and morals can have two different aspects which must be separately assessed.

The first and more conspicuous is the moralization of law, the subordination of law to morals. This is the aspect which is more usually considered, criticised and deplored. It is indeed often alleged as one of the main arguments against natural law and as the reason for its abandonment. Here is a good account of the profound change which has occurred among legal writers in that respect:

"If we compare the juristic writing and judicial decision of the end of the eighteenth century with juristic writing and judicial decision of the end of the nineteenth century, the entire change of front with respect to the nature of law, with respect to the source of obligation of legal precepts, and with respect to the relation of law and morals and consequent relation of jurisprudence and ethics, challenges attention. Thus Blackstone speaks of 'ethics or natural law' as synonymous, and of natural law as the ultimate measure of obligation by which all legal precepts must be tried and from which they derive their whole force and authority. Again, Wilson's lectures on law (delivered in 1790-91 by one of the framers of the federal constitution and a justice of the Supreme Court of the United States) begin with a lecture on the moral basis of legal obligation and a lecture on the law of nature or the universal moral principles of which positive laws are but declaratory.

"In contrast, the institutional book of widest use in English-speaking lands at the end of the nineteenth century (Holland's *Elements of Jurisprudence*) begins with an elaborate setting off of law from 'all rules which, like the principles of morality . . . are enforced by an indeterminate authority' and conceives that natural law is wholly outside of the author's province. Likewise, Mr. Justice Miller, lecturing upon the constitution in 1889-1890, finds no occasion to speak of natural law nor of ethics, but puts a political and historical foundation where Mr. Justice Wilson had put an ethical and philosophical foundation" (POUND, *Law and Morals*, pp. 1-2).

This revulsion against what had been one of the deepest rooted traditions of Western thought—that law is subordinate to morals—is in no way restricted to the English-speaking world. I shall try to show in the next chapter that it is among Continental lawyers that the tendency to strip legal theory of all natural law implications was more clearly developed and carried to its logical conclusions. I am here concerned only with the fact that, to modern eyes, the doctrine of natural law appears to involve a contamination of legality with morality, an obsolete and unacceptable moralization of law. The judgment, if not the blame, is certainly well-founded. The theory of natural law is the outcome of a very old conviction, which goes back to the sources of our civilization : the conviction that the purpose of law is not only to make men obedient, but to help them to be virtuous.

There is, however, another side to the confusion between law and morals. We no longer feel greatly concerned about its consequences, but there was a time when they were a major issue. The introduction of legal valuations into the field of morality can give rise to serious misgivings. Yet the moment we conceive of moral values as expressed in terms of law, as indeed the very notion of natural law requires us to do, it is difficult to see how these misgivings can be avoided. For this can mean only that, in passing judgment on the moral quality of action we do nothing more than pronounce upon the conformity of that action to a legal pattern. If morality consists solely in respect for the law, then the Pharisee is a perfect example of moral behaviour. If moral duties can be couched in legal terms, they can be specified with code-like precision. Casuistry will set in and forecast all possible alternatives. Probabilism will help men to solve their doubts about the most appropriate rule to choose for their conduct. Moral experience is reduced to narrow legal categories. The task of the moralist is for all purposes identical with that of the lawyer. He must expound and interpret the law. Eventually he will also indicate how to employ it with discretion and advantage.

I do not intend to suggest that natural law is entirely responsible for these strange perversions. But it is more than a coincidence that the great age of natural law was also the age of legalistic ethics. And it is significant that Pascal, the bitter enemy of casuistry, was no friend of natural law. In that immortal libel, the *Provinciales* (1657), he denounced *la plaisante comparaison des choses du monde à celles de la con-science*, the "worldliness" which results from the intrusion of legal categories into the field of morality. A truly moral conscience—Pascal pointed out—rebels against the notion that "the rule may be adapted to its subject"; it is not content with probability, but craves for truth. In the same way as the moralization of law was felt to contradict the evidence of legal experience, the legalization of morals was felt to imperil and to destroy the very essence of morality.

It is hardly credible that our forefathers could have been content for so many centuries with the doctrine of natural law if that doctrine had implied and sanctioned such gross mis-conceptions. The truth is, I think, very different. No doubt the fundamental assumption of natural law is the close associ-ation between law and morals. But that assumption allows for a variety of interpretations. The association of morals and law does not rule out the possibility of a demarcation between them. Actually the history of natural law is a history of painstaking efforts to delimit the two spheres and to get to the core of their difference.

The "differential characters" of morals and law are much less of a novelty than its modern supporters would have us believe. What is new is the breach between the two, the assertion that law has nothing to do with morals and that natural law lies wholly outside the province of the lawyer. In fact, the problem of the differentiation between law and morals is so closely associated with the development of political thought that one wonders why it is not given more attention by historians. It coincides with the problem of the purpose and limits of State-action and with the history of political and religious freedom. It was bound to appear under a different light at different stages. The independence of the State had first to be secured against the all-pervading sway of religion

and morality, before the position came to be reversed and the
need to secure the freedom of religious and moral experience
against the encroachments of State action was revealed.

Thus, in a very broad generalization, it might be said that
medieval writers were concerned to prevent morals from
encroaching on law, the writers of the seventeenth and eighteenth
centuries to prevent law from encroaching on morals. But the
problem remained fundamentally the same, and the results of
the efforts to solve it are curiously similar. It is interesting
to compare these results with the full-blown theory of the
"differential characters" of law and morals which is usually
considered as one of the pillars of modern legal philosophy.

I shall restrict my analysis to the best known and more
often quoted of these characters. The first is the "social" or
"objective" character of law as against the "individual" or
"subjective" character of morals. This is how the difference
is defined by one of the exponents of the neo-Kantian school
of legal philosophy:

> "The logical function of law exerts its influence where a
> collision between the acts of two or more agents or an antithesis
> between two or more wills is possible, and tends to promote
> objective ordination among them. The moral criterion, on the
> other hand, supposes an antithesis between two or more possible
> acts of the same agent and tends to settle internal strife, that
> is, to establish a subjective ethical order. From this come the
> diverse elementary characteristics, which delimit the proper
> sphere of each" (DEL VECCHIO, *The Formal Bases of Law*,
> p. 163).

The main idea behind this elaborate language seems to be that
the essential function of law is to make life in society possible.
Ubi societas ibi ius. Law presupposes society. Morals do not.
Moral experience is essentially a matter for the individual.
Legal experience is tied to the notion of a community.

If this is the gist of the first of the so-called "differential
characters," I think that in all fairness we should recognize
that it was not entirely unknown even to the Schoolmen.
Though conceiving of natural law as a moral standard and as
the foundation of all laws, they were careful to draw the line
between such of its applications which refer to men as men,

and those which relate only to men in society. The latter they comprised under the heading of "human law" or law proper; and the justification, and indeed the very essence of human laws, they found in the fact of social relationship. No doubt natural law, as a moral precept, extends to "all acts of virtue". But human laws cover only those aspects of human behaviour which imply a co-ordination with other men. Thus, properly speaking, the laws of men do not primarily aim at promoting virtue, but only at securing a peaceful living together : they do not forbid all that is evil, but only that which imperils society ; they do not command all that is good, but only that which pertains to the general welfare.[1] If the social element in law is conceived as a differential character between law and morals, surely that element was clearly perceived already by medieval legal philosophers.

Another much quoted distinguishing mark of law as opposed to morals is the "coercive" character of legal precepts. The argument is best known to the English reader through Austin's famous enunciation ; but it is certainly much older than Austin and has a long history behind it. According to Kant the "possibility of coercion" is intimately associated with the notion of a legal order. But, as we shall presently see, Kant's deduction of this fundamental aspect of legality goes far beyond the usual acceptance of coercion as a convenient mark by which to distinguish one group of precepts from another.

Here, again, one can only say that, if "sanction" or, to use Austin's words, the "enforcement of obedience", is conceived to be the distinctive attribute of law proper, then even the medieval theorists of natural law had a grasp of the distinction between legal and moral imperatives, in so far as they identified the "discipline of law" with a "discipline which compels under fear of penalty." They actually went so far as to realize that the coercive character of human or positive law is in its essence contradictory to that moral element which the law is supposed to embody.

None the less, what they had in view was not the separation

[1] TH. AQUINAS, *Summa Theol.*, 1a 2ae, 72, 4 ; 96, 2 and 3.

of morals and law, but their unity. All they did was to point out the different binding force of positive as against moral and divine precepts, as well as the fact that the introduction of coercion marks a turning point in the deduction of all laws from the supreme principles of the law of nature.[1]

By far the most important distinction is that between the "external" character of law and the "internal" character of morals. "Externality" was considered by Kant to constitute the very essence of legal experience. But the merit of having "discovered" and formulated the distinction is commonly attributed to Christian Thomasius (1655-1728), a representative like Pufendorf of the German school of natural law, and a champion of freedom of conscience in an age and in a country in which religious intolerance was still a matter of accepted policy.

In his *Fundamenta Iuris Naturae et Gentium* (1705) and in a number of other writings, Thomasius developed the view that the law of the State, as a coercive order, is debarred by its very nature from any action and competence in the sphere of morals. Justice (*iustum*) consists in laying down and respecting the conditions which make human intercourse possible. Its first precept is : "do not unto others what you do not want others to do unto you." But morals, in the widest acceptation (*decorum* and *honestum*), exact much more than that. They imply doing to others what we want others to do to us ; they imply a duty to our own conscience. Legal precepts can therefore be only external ; they can have nothing to do with the inwardness and spontaneity of thought and religion.

Thomasius was drawing the moral of two centuries of religious strife and persecution. His theory lays the foundations of the modern, secular, tolerant State. Its novelty, however, is practical rather than theoretical. The distinction between external and internal obligation, between the *forum externum* and the *forum internum* is not a discovery of Pufendorf or Thomasius. It goes back, if I am not mistaken, to the Canon law. What is new is the sharp distinction between the two, and the assertion that law, and therefore the State, can

[1] TH. AQUINAS, *Summa Theol.*, 1a 2ae, 95, 1 ; 96, 5.

and must have no competence in the *forum internum*, viz., in the "court of conscience". What is new is the belief that it is possible clearly to delimit the sphere which is beyond the bounds of State action, while, on the other hand, cataloguing the commands of the State under the heading of purely external precepts.

But the notion of the inherent disability of positive legislation in matters of thought or religion, is a notion which has its roots in the oldest tradition of Western thought. For it is indeed the essence of Christian belief to stress the intimacy and freedom of moral and religious experience; nor did the "external" character of legal obligation escape the notice of earlier writers on ethics and natural law. Thomas Aquinas and Hooker are in close agreement on this point, stressing as they do that the laws of God work differently from the laws of men:

> "Man, the maker of human law, can pass judgment only upon external action, because 'man seeth those things that appear,' as we are told in the book of *Kings*. God alone, the divine Law-giver, is able to judge the inner movements of the will, as the Psalmist says, 'The searcher of hearts and reins is God'" (TH. AQUINAS, *Summa Theol.*, 1a 2ae, 100, 9).

> "Wherein appeareth also the difference between human and divine laws, the one of which two are content with *opus operatum*, the other require the *opus operantis*, the one but claims the deed, the other especially the mind" (HOOKER, *Eccles. Pol.*, V, lxii, 15).

And long before Aquinas and Hooker, another great Christian writer had given the same thought a solemn expression:

> "The law of God has taught us what to believe, which the laws of men cannot teach us. They can exact a different conduct from those who fear them. But faith they cannot inspire" (ST. AMBROSE, *Ep.* XXI, 10 (Migne, XVI, 1005)).

The conclusion of this short summary is simple. There was a notion of the distinction between law and morals long before the theory of the "differential characters" was fully developed. Far from being responsible for the confusion of the two spheres, the doctrine of natural law led to a better appraisal of their differences. What divides the old school from the new is not so much the confusion between moral and legal obligation as a different view about the position of the State and of law with regard to morals.

The theory of the differential characters is thus at bottom nothing but a political theory, a theory about the nature and limits of State action which was the outcome of a particular historical situation or the expression of a particular ideal that claimed recognition. That this ideal was the outcome of a better understanding of Christian values is, I think, undeniable. But we must be careful not to mistake the effect for the cause, and not to reverse the historical process which led to the formulation of the "differential characters". As Croce ironically remarked, it is not because these characters were suddenly discovered that "the Catholics ceased to bring the Protestants to the stake, and the Protestants to repay them with the same kindness". The differential characters between law and morals were the transformation into a political programme of an ideal which was inherent from the outset in Western civilization. We ought not to forget the blood and the toil which it cost to secure what could henceforward appear as a "neat philosophical theorem".

However, another and deeper criticism of the "differential characters" has been suggested. It must be briefly mentioned because it affords some further arguments for the rehabilitation of the natural law theorists and of their long-forgotten labours. It has been pointed out that these characters, based as they are upon a particular historical experience, can be only approximate and shifting. They cannot survive, on closer inspection, as absolutely valid criteria for distinguishing legal from moral precepts.

Take the social character of law as contrasted with the individual character of morals. It is, of course, true that modern man has come to associate law almost exclusively with the State, and morals almost exclusively with the individual. But are there not moral values which presuppose and foster society as much, if not more, than can the legal order? Are there not laws outside the range of the State, regularly observed and sometimes felt as more binding by the individual? A purely individual morality is unthinkable; and law, if we consider it in its broadest sense as "a rule or measure of action", is ever present in practical experience, even to Robinson Crusoe, who made himself a rule to read the Bible "a while every morning and every night" and to make his way of living as "regular" as possible—thus saving himself from despair and preserving his very humanity.[1]

Nor is the coercive character of certain laws or groups of laws a distinguishing mark of law proper. For one thing, as Lord Bryce pointed out,[2] compulsion is no final explanation of the observance of law, nor is physical force the only type of compulsion. On the other hand, there are a number of laws, that not even the legal positivist would deny to be laws, which lack proper sanctions. Such are, apart from international law, the fundamental laws of a given constitution. The very notion of sanction, it has been pointed out many times, is not quite so simple as Austin would have us believe ; and, at any rate, in the working of law, sanctions have only a complementary function. When a law is infringed, sanctions may operate ; but they cannot succeed in restoring the situation once it has been altered : *factum quod infectum fieri nequit.*

Finally, as far as the external character of law is concerned, nowhere is the approximate character of the distinction more apparent. The valuation of an action as external or internal can never be a matter of general agreement. In our days, the State exacts military service from its citizens, and actually requires them to be good soldiers. In Queen Elizabeth's days, the government enforced Church attendance, but denied the charge of "commanding opinions". Which of the two cases is nearer the notion of law as a purely external command ? How can we prove that law is never concerned with the internal side of action ? What do we make of such legal concepts as *bona fides* or *dolus* which involve a subtle valuation of motives ? What of that "mental element" which plays so decisive and elusive a part in criminal liability ?

Clearly such criticism as this can lead only to the conclusion that the distinction between law and morals should not be based merely on a generalization from our present experience,

[1] DEFOE, *Robinson Crusoe*, sect. X.
[2] *Obedience*, in *Studies in History and Jurisprudence*, Vol. II, 1901.

but on a deeper analysis of the inmost nature of legal and moral obligation. It also leads to the recognition that there must be closer links between the two spheres than is realized *prima facie*. But this brings us back to the position of the theorists of natural law and to a more charitable view of their merits. It is indeed strange enough to discover that much of the criticism which I have summarized can easily be put into traditional natural law language. But it is even more significant to find that the theorists of natural law, because of their very assumption of an indissoluble link between law and morals, have left us some precious evidence for the correct appraisal of their mutual relationship. They may have unduly stressed the moral aspect of law or the legal aspect of morals. But, as has already been shown, they were well aware of the differences between them and showed a surprisingly clear insight into their real nature.

Thus, for example, with regard to the social character of law and the individual character of morals, they would probably have denied that the distinction is as simple as that. Life in society, they would have pointed out, is a moral duty. There is no aspect of life which can be said to be morally indifferent. Moral values tend of necessity to be realized in social, that is, in legal terms. These notions they would have expressed in different ways according to their different inspiration. Aquinas stressed the political nature of man. Grotius was content with an *appetitus societatis*. But the common aim of both the old school of natural law and the new was to emphasize the moral foundation of law as well as the part which law plays in moral experience. The proper scope of justice is "to promote an objective order among men". Justice is therefore essentially *ad alterum*. Yet metaphorically we can speak of justice as present even "in him that leads a solitary life" : for law is nothing but the rule of right reason.[1]

Or take the coercive character of law as opposed to the freedom and spontaneity of morals. We may have good reasons for fearing any doctrine which is based on the assumption that it is the purpose of law to make men "virtuous".

[1] TH. AQUINAS, *Summa Theol.*, 2a 2ae, 58, 2.

But are we so sure that we can, even at the present day, draw a clear line between the precepts which can and cannot, or which should and should not, be enforced by positive legislation ? Are there not many examples of moral duties still forcibly sanctioned by law ? The problem is a different one, and the theorists of natural law saw it clearly. Coercion they fully realized to be contradictory to the moral quality of action. But equally well they realized its inadequacy as an explanation of obedience. The discrimination between morals and law they sought not in the precepts themselves but in their working. Good laws must be obeyed "for conscience sake". It is, therefore, only to evil men that law can appear merely as compulsion.

> "In this sense virtuous and just men are not subject to the law, but only the wicked. For whatever pertains to constraint and to violence is against the will. But the will of the good is at one with the law, whereas in the bad the will is opposed to the law. So, in this sense, the good are not under the law, but only the bad" (TH. AQUINAS, *Summa Theol.*, 1a 2ae, 96, 5).

Here is indeed a very old idea, which goes back to the very sources of Christian teaching. "If ye be led of the Spirit, ye are not under the law" (*Gal.* V, 18). This is not the place to discuss whether its extension from the field of religious to that of moral experience is justified. But the striking analogy certainly throws light upon the real difference between legal and moral obligation. It accounts better than many "sociological" arguments for the basic fact of obedience. Surely not even at the present day does the "good" citizen think of law merely in the shape of the policeman or the law-court. Nor, on the other hand, does he long hesitate to break laws which he deems morally indefensible, at least when he is sure that he can do so with a fair chance of impunity. Is not this the best possible proof that "good" laws are binding *in foro conscientiae* ?

Last, but not least, comes the "external" character of law as opposed to the "internal" character of morals. Once again we find natural law theorists deeply aware of the issue. But when they say, as Hooker says, that laws "but claim the deed" ; or when they emphasize, as Thomas Aquinas emphasizes, that the object of justice is "external operation", they are not taking "externality" in the same way as we do to be a mark by which to fence and delimit the proper field of State action. We can hardly expect them to share our modern views about the comparative claims of religion and politics, nor our notion of the sacred rights of the individual conscience.

I cannot help thinking, however, that both Aquinas and Hooker would probably have been surprised to hear us speak of the modern State as strictly confined to "externals". They would have had little difficulty in pointing out that even in our days opinions are far from being politically irrelevant, and that "purges" are only a more civilized version of the stake. The plain fact is that the demarcation between "externals" and "internals" is as shifting and approximate to-day as it was in the hey-day of natural law theorising. It is difficult to see on what theoretical grounds certain duties which are imposed by the modern State, such as military service, can be described as purely external duties.

Clearly, the distinction cannot lie in the duties as such, but in the manner in which they are imposed and finally fulfilled. And this the old theorists of natural law knew very well, better perhaps than we do. What they had in mind, when they stressed the difference between legal and moral obligation, was that the purpose of law cannot go beyond external conformity. It can enforce virtuous actions, but it cannot secure that these actions should be carried out as they would be by the virtuous man, *eo modo quo virtuosus operatur*.[1] To our efforts to justify conscription in contrast to compulsory Church attendance, they would have objected, I surmise, that whether the law-giver chooses to enjoin the one or the other he will never quite succeed in making a good soldier and even less in making a truly religious man.

All this brings us to a conclusion. We should be more careful not to speak of natural law as a confusion between law and morals. It is undoubtedly true that the very notion of natural law implies their close association. But so does the modern definition of law as an "ethical minimum", which Jellinek made so popular among the jurists.[2] Natural law

---

[1] TH. AQUINAS, *Summa Theol.*, 1a 2ae, 96, 3, ad 2um.
[2] G. JELLINEK, *Die sozialethische Bedeutung von Recht, Unrecht and Strafe*, 1878.

is a vindication of that minimum. But it is not a denial that a distinction between the two spheres of ethics exists and should always be kept in mind for a correct understanding of legal and moral phenomena. In fact, if the theorists of natural law foreshadowed that distinction, they did so not in the empirical terms of a generalization from a given historical situation, but in a truly philosophical sense, as an analysis of the nature of legal and moral obligation. It is possible to find in their now forgotten and discredited speculations a surprisingly clear grasp of the difference between legal conformity and the moral value of action, which one would almost be tempted to relate to Kant's incomparable analysis of the categories of legality and morality.

With Kant the "differential characters" are finally freed from all empirical implications. Kant's deduction of the "external" and "coercive" essence of law represents the conclusion and crown of the long effort to reach a distinction between law and morals. But it also provides the conditions for an entirely new and critical approach to the problems of legal philosophy.

GENERAL LITERATURE

B. CROCE, *Philosophy of the Practical, Economic and Ethic*, 1913.

G. DEL VECCHIO, *The Formal Bases of Law*, 1921.

R. POUND, *Law and Morals*, McNair lectures in the University of N. Carolina, 1924.

C. K. ALLEN, *Legal Duties and other Essays in Jurisprudence*, 1931 (Legal Morality and the *Jus Abutendi*—Legal Duties).

Droit, Morale, Moeurs, II[e] Annuaire de l'Institut International de Philosophie du Droit et de Sociologie Juridique, 1936.

CHAPTER VI

THE IDEAL LAW

I t has been the purpose of this enquiry to show that the theory of natural law provided answers to many problems which still face the modern legal philosopher. No assessment of that theory would, however, be complete without taking into account what may well be said to constitute its most constant feature all through the ages: the assertion of the possibility of testing the validity of all laws by referring them to an ultimate measure, to an ideal law which can be known and appraised with an even greater measure of certainty than all existing legislation. Natural law is the outcome of man's quest for an absolute standard of justice. It is based upon a particular conception of the relationship between the ideal and the real. It is a dualist theory which presupposes a rift, though not necessarily a contrast, between what is and what ought to be.

This must not be taken to mean that the doctrine of natural law is at heart a revolutionary doctrine. Nothing indeed would be more remote from the truth. If natural law played a revolutionary part at certain epochs of Western history, it is equally true that, during most of its age-long development, the doctrine was limited to a mildly progressive, and at times to a frankly conservative function. The recognition of the existence of an ideal law did not necessarily imply that positive law should be overruled by it in cases of conflict. Natural law could serve as well to support revolutionary claims as to justify an existing legal order. It could even lead to the glorification of a particular system of law, as when Roman law, after its reception on the Continent as the "common" law of Europe, came to be considered as the *ratio scripta*, or as when Sir Edward Coke described the English Common law as "nothing else but reason".[1] Justice Holmes humorously described this particular outcome of natural law by remarking:

"It is not enough for the knight of romance that you agree that his lady is a very nice girl—if you do not admit that she is

[1] *The Institutes of the Laws of England*, First Part (1628).

the best that God ever made or will make, you must fight.
There is in all men a demand for the speculative, so much so
that the poor devil who has no other way of reaching it obtains
it by getting drunk. It seems to me that this demand is at the
bottom of the philosopher's effort to prove that truth is absolute
and of the jurist's search for criteria of universal validity which
he collects under the head of natural law" (HOLMES, *Natural
Law*, in "Harvard Law Review," 1918).

This is not a very charitable judgment: but there is no
doubt that natural law was the *belle dame sans merci* who
inspired the crusading spirit of old-time jurisprudence. That
spirit has gone. It has given way to a realistic approach which is
in keeping with an age of prosaic undertakings. The study of
the ideal law is no longer conceived as being of any relevance
to the lawyer. "The juridical science of the nineteenth and
twentieth century expressly declares itself incapable of drawing
the problem of justice into the scope of its enquiries" (Kelsen).
It actually prides itself on being able to master and to construct
into a system any given legal material without resorting to
the delusion of natural law. The abandonment of natural law
marks the rise of modern jurisprudence. This is the fundamental fact which we must keep in mind in order to understand,
if only from a negative angle, what natural law ultimately
stood for. It may well be that after we have examined the
achievements and limitations of modern jurisprudence, the
case for natural law may once again be assessed in a positive
manner.

The rise of modern jurisprudence is marked by the abandonment of natural law and by a new or "positive" approach to
legal experience. But the notion of natural law as the embodiment of justice and as the ultimate ground of the validity of all
laws had been criticized long before the advent of positive
jurisprudence. Nor can the new approach be described as
the outcome of any particular doctrinal standpoint. The word
"positivism", if one cares to use it in this connection, can indicate only an attitude rather than a definite philosophical creed.
Indeed, the oldest argument against natural justice is the
sceptical argument. It goes back to the very beginnings of
speculative thought. It has a long history which stretches

down from the Sophists to the present day. I need only refer the reader, for a classical treatment of the subject, to Hume's *Treatise of Human Nature*, Book II, part ii, or to the section in Cicero's *Republic* (III, vi-xx), where Carneades' argument is set forth with sufficient vigour and clearness to remind us how little there is that can be called entirely new in legal and political philosophy.

Modern or positive jurisprudence is not necessarily based upon scepticism, nor does it imply a denial that the problem of justice exists. Modern jurists may be willing to leave the discussion of the ultimate reason why law should be regarded as binding to the legal philosopher, without taking a definite stand about the existence of natural law. Nor do they accept as a matter of course the "monist" view of the coincidence of the ideal and the real which, as we have seen in a preceding chapter, consecrated the law of the State as the embodiment of ethical values. All they do is to put the problem of the ideal or natural law, as it were, within brackets. However influenced they may have been or still are by one or other philosophical current, their implicit or explicit philosophy is not the determining factor. They are indeed anxious to convince us that theirs is not a philosophical, but a "scientific" concern.

This, I understand, is apparent among English jurists. To the foreign observer English jurisprudence—with some notable exceptions—may still seem to have a flavour of utilitarianism as a distinctive national characteristic. And indeed, if we think of Austin, we may well believe that the cradle of modern English jurisprudence was utilitarian philosophy. But Austin himself, if I am not mistaken, was careful not to tie his notion of jurisprudence to any particular philosophical assumption. He actually avoided any final pronouncement on the possibility of evaluating legal experience from a standpoint other than that of the "analytical" jurist. Of general jurisprudence he wrote :

"It is concerned directly with principles and distinctions which are common to various systems of particular or positive law ; and which each of these various systems inevitably involves, let it be worthy of praise or blame, or let it accord or not with an assumed measure or test" (AUSTIN, *Lectures*, Campbell's ed., I, 33).

He seems clearly to admit that "the goodness or badness of laws" might be tried "by the test of utility (or by any of the various tests which divide the opinions of mankind)". He contented himself with declaring that with this kind of under-taking general jurisprudence "has no immediate concern". The problem of the ideal law is neither denied nor declared insoluble. It is simply put within brackets as irrelevant to the task of the jurist.

Very similar remarks can be made about Continental jurisprudence. This was, as is well known, the outcome of the "Historical school", and it is significant that the standard-bearer of that school—F. C. von Savigny (1779-1861)—was also the founder, or at any rate the most authoritative exponent, of the systematic treatment of law which still obtains general recognition and application in the law-schools of the Continent. Now the Historical school—the programme of which was laid down in Savigny's famous book, published in 1814, *Of the Vocation of Our Age for Legislation and Jurisprudence*—meant, if not a new philosophical theory of law, at least the manifestation in the field of law of a great philosophical revolution. It was an aspect as well as a result of the great tide of Romanticism which, foreshadowed in the eighteenth century, swept Europe as a counterblow to the French revolution.

As its name clearly indicates, the Historical school was essentially a vindication of growth and development against the abstract rationalism which had become the distinguishing mark of natural law theory in its last stage of development. It stressed that the origin and the explanation of legal phenomena must not be sought in the individual, but in collective life ; that law is the product of the particular genius of each nation (*Volksgeist*) ; that legal experience should not be arrested and as it were crystallized in statutes and codes, but allowed to grow and bear fruit in its full vigour and vitality.

How then can it be explained that the untiring advocate of the historical study of law should also have been the exponent fo a systematic treatment which seems to be mainly inspired by the rationalist quest for order, coherence and unity? Savigny's *System of Present-day Roman Law* (1840-49) brought to perfection a method which had long been applied, in Germany and elsewhere, in the study of the common (Roman) law of Continental Europe. It added little or nothing to the pattern that the great *Pandektisten* had elaborated, which had come to be considered as the necessary introductory or "general" part (*Allgemeiner Teil*) of jurisprudence. Under that heading the notions of law, objective and subjective right, juridical relationship, personality, facts, things and so forth, had been abstractly assessed and defined. These notions have remained down to the present day the elements of legal study and training on the Continent.

Now it might well be questioned whether the acceptance by Savigny of any of these abstract categories was not in contradiction to the notion of law which he championed. These categories were derived from the essentially individualistic conception of law which had inspired the Continental law-schools for centuries. Surely they needed recasting if they were to be fitted to a new conception of law as the expression of the organic life of society. It must also be remembered that the final outcome of the Historical school, as Sir Ernest Barker has pointed out,[1] was a vindication of "national" law (in the particular case of Germany, of German law) as against Roman law, the impact of which was bound to be more and more resented as alien. The "Germanist" doctrine of group-personality, the "organic theory of the State", the struggle against individualism in the field of public and even of private law, all trace their beginnings to the Historical school.

But the point which must here receive our attention is the paradox of the parallel birth of the historical interpretation of law and of modern, positive jurisprudence. The Historical school had begun by stressing the growth and development of law, it ended by fostering its scientific study. It had begun with an apology for history. It ended with an apology for jurisprudence. The paradox is worth considering more

---

[1] Introduction to GIERKE, *Natural Law and the Theory of Society* pp. liv-lv.

closely, for it is one of the crucial episodes in the rise of modern juristic thought, and it throws light upon its fundamental nature.

The explanation of the riddle can be found only in the correct interpretation of Savigny's intentions, as well as of the real aims and purposes of the historical doctrine. Already in the *Vocation* Savigny had pointed out that the life of law is, as it were, twofold. Law has a "political" life inasmuch as it expresses the realities of a given social structure. But law has also a "technical" life, which begins the very moment it undergoes its "scientific" elaboration at the hands of the jurist.[1] Law is no doubt the product of the *Volkgeist* and the outcome of history. But it can be assessed and appraised only through the labours of the professional lawyer.

The complete change of front from the old natural law approach is here apparent. The rationalist school had led to an exaltation of the law-giver as the agent for the realization of justice. The Historical school led to an exaltation of the jurist as the interpreter of historical growth and development. But this does not mean that the followers of the Historical school intended to substitute historical growth and development for the notion of absolute justice. Its greatest representatives, such as Savigny, Puchta and Stahl, remained unshaken in their Christian belief in an order of justice based upon the existence of a transcendent God. They must not be mistaken for Hegelians. Theirs was at bottom a "dualist" theory : they never accepted the fundamental assumption of Hegel's legal philosophy, that the ideal finds its revelation in history. The cult of history they had in common with all the Romantics. But historicism was a method to them, rather than a philosophy. They, too, were putting the ideal law within brackets. Jurisprudence was called in to fill the vacuum.

It filled it so well and so thoroughly that, for a time, the old quest for the ideal law seemed to have been written off from the tasks of the jurist and the lawyer. The achievement of nineteenth century jurisprudence is a great and positive

[1] F. C. von SAVIGNY, *Of the Vocation of Our Age for Legislation and Jurisprudence*, transl. by Hayward, 1831, pp. 22-29, 62.

one. The age of science produced a science of law worthy of its ambitions. Anyone who is acquainted with the immense amount of ingenuity which generation after generation of jurists spent in constructing the majestic edifice of modern jurisprudence, cannot easily believe that such labours could have been in vain.

To bring order, coherence and unity into the system of law, to provide the law-giver with a clear map of his province, the lawyer and the judge with a body of concepts which should enable them to perform their duties with the greatest amount of precision and ease : this was, for nearly a century, the distinguishing mark of legal theory on the Continent. And it is indeed on the Continent rather than in English-speaking countries that Austin's programme of a "general jurisprudence" has been carried out to the full. "As principles abstracted from positive systems are the subject of general jurisprudence, so is the exposition of such principles its exclusive or appropriate object." German *Rechtswissenschaft*, with its relentless pursuit of an ever-increasing degree of systematic perfection and of formal abstraction, can and must be taken as the best illustration of the fate of legal theory after the spell of natural law had been broken.

This is not the place to discuss the character and value of legal science, or, if we may indeed identify the two terms, of modern jurisprudence : its claim, that is, to possess the character of a science, as well as the possibility of its universal application. These are not two different problems, but one : for indeed, if we admit the claim of jurisprudence to be " the formal science of positive law"—as Holland defined it—I can see no reason why we should not admit that jurisprudence may be "particular" or "general" according to the greater or lesser degree of induction and generalization which has been performed in the collection and elaboration of legal material. If jurisprudence is an empirical science, then clearly it is so from beginning to end, nor is there any substantial change, either in its methods or in its results, whether it restricts itself to the *Dogmatik* or scientific elaboration of a particular legal order, or whether it progresses to a "general theory of law" (*Allgemeine Rechtslehre*) which "takes up . . . several systems of law and seeks for legal institutions which have appeared in history on more than one occasion" (Stammler).

What I am concerned with here is a different question. It is the claim of modern jurisprudence to have entirely eliminated the problems which had for centuries been considered and discussed under the heading of the natural or ideal law, the claim to self-sufficiency, if I may so call it, of modern jurisprudence, viz., to provide the student of the law with the sufficient and necessary criteria for the understanding and interpretation of legal phenomena. In order to assess to what extent that claim is justified we must now examine the answer which modern jurisprudence has given to the problem of the validity of the laws which are the object of its study.

The existence of that problem was certainly never denied by the "positive" jurist. On the contrary, it is because it purported to restrict itself only to the study of laws "actually valid" that modern jurisprudence was led to lay all the emphasis on the adjective "positive". That term can have a meaning only as a term of contrast. "There is no law but positive law", wrote Stahl[1]; natural law precepts "possess neither the requisite definiteness nor the binding force of law". But Bergbohm, the "diligent tracker of natural law", was perfectly right to point out that, from the point of view of legal positivism, the very use of the adjective "positive" with regard to law is nothing but a pleonasm.[2]

The real question was to determine which laws are sufficiently "definite", or "binding", or "positive" to deserve the name of laws. It is on this point that the difficulties began, and that the peculiarities of legal empiricism soon became apparent. It gradually dawned upon lawyers and jurists that the validity or "positiveness" of law cannot consist, or at least cannot consist solely, in the mere fact of its enforcement. The use of force, or the possibility of its use, is only the outward or material aspect of positive law. From a strictly juridical or "formal" point of view the validity of a particular law cannot depend upon its varying degree of effectiveness. It consists in

---

[1] F. J. STAHL, quot. by H. ROMMEN, *The Natural Law*, p. 117.
[2] K. BERGBOHM, *Jurisprudenz und Rechtsphilosophie*, I, 1892, p. 49, 51 ff.

the fact that that particular law belongs to a system which is singled out and recognized as the only positive and valid system.

That this system, to nineteenth century jurists, was the system or legal order of the State, has only a relative importance. The formal or logical side of their argument is the side which calls for attention. To say that the positiveness of law derives from its belonging to a positive system is in fact only a different way of saying that the recognition of its validity as a law depends on the possibility of referring it back, directly or indirectly, to a common source from which all legal precepts ultimately proceed. This is what the jurists, borrowing an old term with which we are already acquainted, indicated under the name of sovereignty. Sovereignty became the sacred dogma of positive jurisprudence, because it was the condition of the positiveness of law. Sovereignty may be, and indeed is, a fact. But from the juridical angle it was also, and essentially, a formal criterion : the criterion which made it possible to recognize a rule or a body of rules as part of a positive order, and therefore to pronounce on their validity as laws.

Thus the restriction of all law to positive law and the quest for a systematic construction of the legal order went hand in hand. They are indeed the two fundamental aspects of modern jurisprudence. Its tendency to become more and more "formal" was only a consequence of its purpose to be a "positive" science, that is, to steer clear of any criterion of validity of law—such as natural law—extraneous to the system.

We have of late grown accustomed to consider this "formal" character of jurisprudence as self-evident. I have no doubt that we are greatly indebted to the "pure theory of law", developed by Kelsen and his school, for a sounder appreciation of the logical issues of the juristic method. But the process which led modern jurisprudence to an increasing degree of abstraction had long been at work. It is interesting to look back upon it and to see how the concepts which had at first provided the basis of positive jurisprudence were gradually transformed, as it were by an internal logic. The process is curiously reminiscent of the old discussions about the essence of law which have been examined in a preceding chapter.

Positive jurisprudence had started from the identification of law and command. It ended with the elimination of will from the field of law altogether. This is apparent not only in the sphere of "public law", in the untiring efforts of "classical" German jurisprudence (Jellinek, Laband, etc.) to construe the State as a *Rechtsstaat*. It is equally apparent in the sphere of "private law", as anyone can easily gather who is acquainted with the great debate on the *Willenstheorie* which divided nineteenth century jurists.

The tendency was to eliminate any intrinsic, original power of the will, whether of the State or of the individual. To admit such a power, it was argued, is nothing but a natural law proposition : for where can will derive its juridical value from except from law itself ? Surely, if we admit, as Savigny admitted, a "natural capacity" of the human person to set in motion legal consequences ; or if we ascribe, as Windscheid ascribed, a "creative force" to the individual will in laying down legal precepts, we deprive State sovereignty of its essential function as the ultimate source of all rules which have positive validity.

In turn, even sovereignty is a misnomer. It seems to indicate that the will of a man or of a body of men is endowed with some original legal value—a natural law proposition ! From a purely juridical, that is, from a strictly "formal" and "positive" standpoint, it is clear that the will of this or that man or body of men is creative of law only because there is a superior law (the law of the constitution) which attributes to that will a juridical relevance.

The tendency among up-to-date writers is in fact to substitute some other expression for the word "sovereignty", wherever it would have been used in the past. Thus we hear it now said that the legal order can be conceived only as "complete" and "exclusive". Exclusive, because the recognition of a particular legal order as positive implies that the rules which compose it are, for the jurist, the only valid ones : all other rules are not properly laws but mere facts.[1] Complete,

---

[1] This principle has been applied with remarkable success in the theory of Conflict of Laws, or Private International Law, as it is called on the Continent.

because the admission that there may be "gaps" in the law is nothing but a delusion, which springs from the belief that there may be situations or facts "intrinsically" juridical—a residue of natural law thinking. From a really "positive" standpoint, unless these situations or facts are given relevance by a law, they are, as far as the legal order is concerned, simply non-existent.

We seem to be forced to the conclusion that command is not the essential attribute of law. The function of law is to qualify, to provide, as it were, a term of reference for certain situations and facts by ascribing a particular meaning to them, or inserting them in a relation of condition and sequence. The widespread adoption of the word "norm" in modern juristic terminology is, from this point of view, particularly significant. For that word does, it is true, involve the notion of an "ought", but also and primarily that of a standard or model or pattern ; and the "injunctive" character is at any rate in no way essential to an "ought" proposition. Thus, modern legal thought has been led to emphasize more and more the logical character of law, and to conceive of juridical categories as mere symbols or names for indicating the relevance of certain situations and facts from a given "normative" angle. The parallel between law and language is ready to hand, as well as the comparison of jurisprudence and grammar.[1]

This description of the characteristics of modern legal thought may sound strange to English ears. The tendencies which I have described may perhaps be suspected as fundamentally alien. Jurisprudence on this side of the Channel has preserved a solid core of commonsense which has guarded it from the perils of over-abstraction. It may also be doubted whether all the conclusions of Continental juristic thinking are applicable to a type of legal experience such as that of the Common law, entirely different from the tradition of Roman law on the Continent.[2]

[1] See below, pp. 119-120.
[2] For the "typically English approach" to the problems of legal theory I need only refer the reader to Professor GOODHART'S recent and most stimulating lecture, *English Contributions to the Philosophy of Law*, New York, 1949.

There is, however, one point which of late has attracted attention in England also. I would like to refer to it as one of the best illustrations of the final outcome of present-day legal theory, as well as one of the most carefully thought-out attempts to provide an answer to the problem of the validity of law which, as I have pointed out, was from the outset one of the inspiring motifs of positive jurisprudence. It is the notion of the "basic norm", which Kelsen and his followers have stressed as the necessary presupposition for a systematic construction of the legal order. The notion is well known, and readily understood in the light of what has already been said about the logical issues of the juristic method.

The "basic norm" is, according to Kelsen, the condition of completeness and self-sufficiency in a given legal order— in other words, of its "positiveness". "The basic norm of a legal order is the postulated ultimate rule according to which the norms of this order are established and annulled, receive and lose their validity." "The quest for the reason of validity of a norm is not—like the quest for the cause of an effect—a *regressus ad infinitum ;* it is terminated by a highest norm which is the last ground of validity within the normative system." In other words, the basic norm is the necessary hypothesis on which the jurist sets to work : his first and primary task is indeed that of discovering the common ground of validity in each and every norm or group of norms which constitute the system.

This, Kelsen maintains, is possible for any given legal material : for the determination of the basic norm "implies no categorical statement as to the value of the method of law-making or of the person functioning as the positive legal authority ; this value is a hypothetical assumption". Thus the basic norm of national law in the modern sovereign State is that the commands of the sovereign (a man or a body of men) are to be obeyed ; the basic norm of the international legal order is that *pacta sunt servanda*, and so forth. Each and every order will appear as a hierarchical system, every part of which derives from the basic norm its ultimate ground of validity.

I can see no serious objection to Kelsen's theory of the

"basic norm" as the condition of correct legal thinking. On the contrary, I think that the theory throws considerable light upon the real nature of jurisprudence. In grounding his whole construction upon a hypothetical premise, the jurist may well claim that he is doing nothing but what is done in all other empirical sciences. But what should always be borne in mind is that scientific constructions are based upon "working" hypotheses. The fundamental task is therefore for the scientist to choose his hypothesis correctly. The moment it ceases to work, the question of rejecting it arises, and of superseding it with another and better one.

I find it difficult to see how the jurist who accepts the postulates of the "pure theory of law" for what they are worth —as an admirable system of formal logic applied to the law[1] — can avoid asking himself some similar question. The basic norm of a national system of law—that the commands of the sovereign are to be obeyed—can have a meaning for the jurist (who will then be able to declare that the system is a positive system) only inasmuch as the commands of the sovereign are in fact obeyed. Similarly, the basic norm of international law, *pacta sunt servanda*, can provide the foundation of the international order only inasmuch as there is such an order in which *pacta sunt servata*: which is, I suppose, what international lawyers, from Grotius onwards, have, correctly or incorrectly, assumed.

In other words there is, and must be, a point at which the basic norm—the hypothesis—is converted into a fact—a thesis—unless its validity be derived from some other or further hypothesis, from a norm which will no longer be positive but can only be a proposition of "natural law", a pronouncement on justice.

Thus, in its latest and most up-to-date developments, modern jurisprudence has really done nothing more than shift to a higher plane the old problem which used to be discussed under the heading of the ideal or natural law. The following quotation from Kelsen seems to me particularly significant :

"That a norm of the kind just mentioned is the basic norm

[1] H. J. LASKI, *Grammar of Politics*, 4th ed., p. vi.

of the national legal order does not imply that it is impossible to go beyond that norm. Certainly one may ask why one has to respect the first constitution as a binding norm. The answer might be that the fathers of the first constitution were empowered by God. The characteristic of so-called legal positivism is, however, that it dispenses with any such religious justification of the legal order. The basic norm is only the necessary presupposition of any positivistic interpretation of legal material" (KELSEN, *General Theory of Law and State*, p. 116).

How this passage reveals the Achilles' heel of modern legal positivism ! For the recognition that the ultimate test of the validity of law lies *beyond* law itself is nothing but a natural law proposition. In peaceful days, when the actual observance of law (be it of the commands of the State or of treaties solemnly entered upon) was unchallenged, "positivism" could find in "facts" its ground and perhaps its justification. But the moment "facts" are called into question, the moment a "choice" must be made between two or more possible alternatives,[1] I can see no reason why the old argument of natural law, which purported to value the facts and to direct the choice, should not be reconsidered.

The typically German dilemma of either blind force or blind faith with which Kelsen leaves us stranded can never be entirely satisfactory. Positivism may indeed dispense with the quest for the ultimate foundation of the legal order. But this makes it entirely powerless when a vital issue is involved, such as the defence or the destruction of that order. It is tragically significant that the country where formal jurisprudence was developed to its utmost perfection was also the country where legality offered least resistance to the challenge of new and disruptive forces. Events seem to have brought us back once again to long forgotten responsibilities.

I would like to conclude this long argument with the mention of some recent examples of the inadequacy of legal positivism to solve the problem of the ultimate validity of law. Examples

---

[1] Kelsen gives an example of such an alternative in the case of the relationship between national and international law. The choice between the two hypotheses of the "primacy" of the one or the other he declares to be merely a matter of " political ideology."

of this kind are, in our troubled days, only too frequent. I remember a time, not very remote, when there was in my country not one but four different legal orders, all of which could have claimed some degree of "positiveness". I prefer to use a simpler example which was given by Professor Goodhart in a recent article.[1]

A statute is promulgated during the war by the Netherlands Government in London, purporting to bind Dutch subjects in Holland. Professor Goodhart asks "is this law?"—by which he means, I presume, "is it positive law?", law the validity of which can be ascertained by the criteria of positive jurisprudence. Now, as Professor Goodhart points out, the statute was certainly a law from the point of view of the Netherlands Government, who regarded themselves as having the right to issue it, independently of the fact whether it could ever be made efficacious. Yet, on the other hand, the German authorities would never have regarded it as a law, not even if every citizen in Holland had obeyed it. From the standpoint of a third party, such as the British courts, the question might have been dubious. "The real difficult question arises, however, when we consider the position of the inhabitant of Holland."

Professor Goodhart suggests that, at the end of the war, the Netherlands courts would have considered his particular views as immaterial. They would have confined themselves to assessing the actual observance or violation of the statute. And, indeed, so they should according to "positive" jurisprudence. But, as Professor Goodhart frankly admits, "this does not mean that the view of the individual is unimportant. On the contrary, a large part of political history has been concerned with disputes between individuals and governments regarding the authority of the latter to declare law."

I submit that what Professor Goodhart seems to consider a political issue is what our benighted ancestors would have called a clear issue of natural law. I submit that this issue can be solved only on the traditional lines of calling the validity of positive law into question, and that it is impossible for the

[1] *An Apology for Jurisprudence*, in *Interpretations of Modern Legal Philosophies*, 1947.

individual to do so unless he decides on the justice of the law which he is asked to obey. But I further submit that it is possible to find in quite recent developments of legal theory and practice a clear indication of a return to the obsolete notions which positivism had criticised and declared to be unacceptable.

That the whole question of the trial of war criminals at the end of the war would raise a "natural law" issue was an authoritative opinion which events have fully confirmed.[1] No doubt the provisions for the Nürnberg Tribunal were based, or purported to be based, on existing or "positive" international law. Apart from the preliminary and controversial question of individual responsibility under international law, the violation of international treaties, of the laws and customs of war, and above all of Article I of the Preamble to the Fourth Hague Convention of 1907 (the "Martens clause" which formally included the "laws of humanity" and the "dictates of the public conscience" within the boundaries of international law) certainly provided a "positive" basis for the prosecution.

But I strongly suspect that the boundaries of legal positivism were overstepped, and had to be overstepped, the moment it was stated that the trials were a "question of justice". The principle *nullum crimen sine poena*, on which the sentences were grounded, was a flat contradiction of one of the most generally accepted principles of positive jurisprudence, the principle *nulla poena sine lege*. Whether or not the assertion of that principle constitutes a dangerous precedent is not for me to judge. All I suggest is that the words used by the Court ("So far from it being unjust to punish him, it would be unjust if his wrong were allowed to go unpunished"[2]) are clearly reminiscent of old natural law argumentations. The rejection of the defence of superior orders makes that reminiscence even more poignant : for it is nothing less than the old doctrine that the validity of laws does not depend on their

---

[1] LORD WRIGHT, *Natural Law and International Law* (*Interpretations of Modern Legal Philosophies*, 1947) ; *War Crimes under International Law* ("Law Quart. Review", 1946).

[2] *The Times*, 1t October, 1946.

"positiveness", and that it is the duty of the individual to pass judgment on laws before he obeys them.

Thus, after a century of effort to eliminate the dualism between what is and what ought to be from the field of legal and political experience, natural law seems to have taken its revenge upon the very champions of the pernicious doctrine that there is no law but positive law, or that might equals right, since for all practical purposes the two propositions are perfectly equivalent.

GENERAL LITERATURE

R. POUND, *Outline of Lectures on Jurisprudence*, 5th ed., 1943 (a complete bibliographical guide).

SIR P. VINOGRADOFF, *Common-sense in Law*, 10th impr., 1933.

C. K. ALLEN, *Jurisprudence—What and Why?* in *Legal Duties*, 1931

Modern Theories of Law, ed. by J. JENNINGS, 1933.

J. W. JONES, *Historical Introduction to the Theory of Law*, 1940.

W. FRIEDMANN, *Legal Theory*, 1944.

W. W. BUCKLAND, *Some Reflections on Jurisprudence*, 1945.

G. W. PATON, *A Text-Book of Jurisprudence*, 1946.

J. STONE, *The Province and Function of Law*, 1946.

H. KELSEN, *General Theory of Law and State*, 1946, with an Appendix on *Natural Law Doctrine and Legal Positivism*.

Interpretations of Modern Legal Philosophies, Essays in honour of Roscoe Pound, 1947.

A useful selection from authors can be found in J. HALL's *Readings in Jurisprudence*.

For the interpretation of Savigny, which is outlined in this chapter, I wish to acknowledge my indebtedness to an excellent Italian book by G. SOLARI, *Storicismo e diritto privato*, 1940.

For a further analysis of "formal" jurisprudence and for a survey of the immense literature on the subject, I must refer to my book, *Il Negozio Giuridico*, 1934.

Mention should be made here of the remarkable efforts made by French jurisprudence to disentangle itself from the impact of positivism. Under the influence especially of Gény (*Science et technique en droit privé positif*, 1914-1924), a renaissance of natural law thinking has taken place among French legal writers which could well be the object of a separate study.

CONCLUSION

THE time has now come to bring this long argument to a tentative conclusion. The validity of that conclusion can be tested only by the light which it throws upon the problem at issue. A great jurist of the last century who devoted his life to the historical study of law, once wrote that the undying spirit of natural law can never be extinguished. "If it is denied entry into the body of positive law, it flutters around the room like a ghost and threatens to turn into a vampire which sucks the blood from the body of law."[1] The present essay is an attempt to account for the ghost and perhaps to exorcise it.

I suggested at the beginning of this enquiry that we should try to assess the meaning of natural law from two different angles, the historical and the philosophical. But on closer inspection these two lines of approach cannot but appear as fundamentally contradictory. The very notion of an "historical function" is hardly compatible with that of a "permanent value". History may well tell us the part which the doctrine of natural law has played in the building up of our cultural heritage. It may convince us of the importance of spiritual factors in the shaping of events and of positive institutions. But it will also make us painfully aware of the "relativism" of all natural law theories. It will provide the unfriendly critic with further grounds for dismissing such theories as typical "ideological superstructures" in the interplay and clash of historical forces.

Political ideology is the term which modern historians tend to substitute whenever natural law would formerly have been mentioned. From a strictly historical standpoint the two expressions may well seem equivalent. As the former Master of Balliol once pointed out, even the doctrine which, at the present day, most emphatically claims to be based on a "scientific" interpretation of history, can easily be construed into a theory of natural right.[2] Yet, on the other hand, the

[1] O. von GIERKE, *Natural Law and the Theory of Society*, I, p. 226.
[2] A. D. LINDSAY, *K. Marx's Capital*, An Introductory Essay, 1925.

113

champions of historical relativism (of which Marxism, if I inter
pret it correctly, is certainly an aspect) will have little difficult
in showing that the most solemn assertions of "natural rights"—
such as, to take one of the more recent examples, the *Universa
Declaration of Human Rights*, adopted on Dec. 10, 1948, b
the General Assembly of United Nations in Paris—are nothin
but ideological programmes, or indeed war machines, to b
used and tested in the battlefield of history.[1]

The question then is, whether the historical explanatio
of the notion of natural law can be accepted as the fina
explanation. In that case the proper place for its assessmen
is the history of political thought rather than the study o
legal philosophy. My contention is, that legal philosoph
also has something to say on the subject, and that a notion whic
has proved to be constructive and valuable to man has a clain
to be assessed not only *sub specie historiae* but *sub specie aeterni*

This obviously presupposes a particular view of th
function of legal philosophy, and may seem to bring us on t
highly controversial ground—for on what indeed do legal philo
sophers agree except on the most conventional platitudes ?
I shall assume that they agree at least on the existence of
fundamental problem : the problem *quid ius* ?—"what is law ?
which, as Kant pointed out, puts the jurist in the same
embarrassment in which the logician is put by the question
"what is truth ?"[3] I believe that the doctrine of natural law i
nothing less than an attempt to answer that question, and tha
this attempt provides the explanation of the constant return o
natural law, as well as the only constant feature of natural law
thinking.

As an answer to the problem *quid ius* ? natural law is, firs
and foremost, a rejection of all empirical solutions, such a

---

[1] The volume *Human Rights*, A Symposium, recently published by
UNESCO (1949), provides the best running commentary on the fundamental "conflict of ideologies" which underlies the compromise finally
agreed upon in the U.N. Declaration.

[2] For a description of the "function" of legal philosophy see POUND,
An Introduction to the Philosophy of Law, 4th printing, 1930, Chapter I,
where the close connection between natural law thinking and philosophical
speculation about law is aptly illustrated.

[3] Kant, *Einleitung in die Rechtslehre*, Sect. B.

purport to derive the notion of law from a process of induction ever more generalized and extended. Kant compared a "purely empirical theory of law" to "the wooden head in Phædrus' fable, which may be beautiful, but alas! has no brain".

Kant was indeed the most forceful exponent of natural law theory in modern days, when he maintained that the jurist should turn "to pure reason for the source of his judgments in order to provide a foundation for all possible legislation". But he is also the most coherent and persuasive critic of legal empiricism when he points out that knowledge of what the laws actually "say or have said" will never enable the jurist to know what law *is*, but only what *pertains to* the law (*quid iuris*) in a given place and at a given time. I think that the survey which has been made in the preceding chapter of the aims and methods of modern legal science provides a striking confirmation of such criticism.

Yet, on the other hand, the notion of natural law has nothing in common with the theories which some modern legal philosophers, claiming the authority of Kant, have put forward as an answer to the question *quid ius* : viz., that the notion of law is a purely logical category, which may enable us to recognize the existence of law but not to pronounce on its goodness or badness. I gravely doubt whether any of the greatest natural law theorists—from Cicero to Kant—would have accepted the neo-Kantian distinction between the "concept" and the "ideal" of law. To them, the concept and the ideal coincided. Theirs would never have been merely a theory of *richtiges Recht*. It was the *gerechtes Recht* they were after.[1] Natural law was indeed to them the supreme "legal category". It enabled them to "distinguish" or identify law within the indistinct mass of practical human experience. But it "valued" as well as it "distinguished". To the question *quid ius* ? the theorists of natural law unanimously answered *ius quia iustum*.

---

[1] The distinction between *richtig* (correct) and *gerecht* (just) as applied to law (*Recht*) was a favourite theme of the neo-Kantians. It was intended to correspond to the two different angles—the logical and the moral—from which the problem of law can be viewed.

Thus the doctrine of natural law is in fact nothing but an assertion that law is a part of ethics. I do not think that this judgment can be seriously challenged from the historical side, though I am willing to admit that the "ethical" character of law may have been stressed to a greater or lesser extent by different writers. I suggest that we look a little more deeply into the full implications of the assertion.

In order to provide a satisfactory answer to the question *quid ius*, the proposition *ius quia iustum* certainly requires some further qualification. It obviously can not be merely a question of definition, nor of carving out, as it were, a particular slice of experience which we agree to indicate by the name of law according to definition. It is further necessary to account for that very experience, to explain not only *what* laws are, but *why* they exist, the reasons which make legal phenomena an inevitable aspect of human life and behaviour. I have no doubt that for Kant the question "what is law?" really meant "how is law possible at all?" (*wie ist Recht überhaupt möglich?*). I am not here concerned with Kant's "transcendental" deduction of ethics. I am rather concerned with the possibility of testing the old doctrine of natural law from this modern and critical standpoint.

I submit that the doctrine can stand the test successfully. For if we admit that the very assertion of natural law is an assertion that law is a part of ethics, its essential function can appear only as that of mediating between the moral sphere and the sphere of law proper. The notion of natural law partakes at the same time of a legal and of a moral character. Perhaps the best description of natural law is that it provides a name for the point of intersection between law and morals. Whether such a point of intersection exists is therefore the ultimate test of the validity of all natural law thinking.

Now the existence of such a point can to my mind hardly be denied when we look at the question from the purely legal angle. I need not remind the reader of the conclusions reached in the preceding chapter. That a strictly empirical treatment of law, such as that which modern jurisprudence purports to achieve, ultimately leads to a problem which the positive jurist is unable to solve, is all that need be admitted. It may be bjected that this problem is not necessarily a "moral" problem, nd that the linking up of a given legal system either to the actual existence of sovereignty, or to the recognition of a particular political ideology, is the best guarantee of the final elimination of the "moral" element, of the "metaphysical" notion of natural law from the theory of positive law.

But let us not be deceived by such sham substitutions. The "factual" existence of sovereignty can provide a convenient peg for the jurist only inasmuch as he accepts the equation of might and right as a final proposition. And as for "political ideologies", they are only too clearly an assertion of values ; nor does the relativism in which they are cloaked, and the "emotional aura" they foster, alter their fundamentally moral (or immoral) character. Natural law they resemble as Satan resembles God. These bloodthirsty idols are proving to be far more exacting than the old gods of truth and of justice. Such doctrines at any rate purport to provide us with judgments on the goodness or badness of laws. And the goodness or badness of laws is obviously a matter which pertains to the moral sphere proper.

Now let us look at the same problem from the other, the moral, angle. Natural law was an endeavour to formulate in legal or "normative" terms certain fundamental values which were believed to be absolutely valid. With this claim to absolute validity I am not here concerned. It is the task of the moralist to assess it. But I would like to call the reader's attention to the notion that values must be given a "normative" expression in order to have a meaning. We are told by recent analysts that the sentence "this is good" has a "meaning" only as expressing an attitude or as an incitement to action.[1] Natural-law theorists would probably have agreed, though on very different grounds and for totally different purposes. They stressed the necessity of translating the notion of "good" into the precept "do good and avoid evil", and this, they maintained, is the first generative proposition of natural law, and hence of all legal precepts.

This really amounts to a recognition of the "inevitability"

[1] OGDEN and RICHARDS, *The Meaning of Meaning*, 4th ed., 1936, p. 125.

of legal or normative propositions in the field of practical experience. Taken in this, the broadest sense possible, laws are nothing but the outcome of the quest for clear and definite standards of valuation whenever action is involved. This is perhaps the place to recall Vico's profound remark about the *verum* and the *certum* in law. The "truth" of the laws—according to the Italian philosopher—is the moral value which they embody, "the light and splendour of natural reason". But the moral element in law must not blind us to its other and necessary aspect, the crude appearance which values assume when they are embodied in positive legislation, when they are "particularized" or cashed, as it were, in a system of authoritative precepts.

"The certainty of laws involves an obscuring of reason, in so far as in them reason is supported merely by authority. And this makes us experience the laws as hard to obey, and yet we are constrained to obey them because of their being certain" (VICO, *Scienza Nuova Seconda* (1744), CXI, CXIII).

If these considerations be granted, perhaps we may have an argument to persuade both the jurist and the moralist that the old speculations about natural law were not entirely purposeless.

The jurist is the man of the *certum*. It is right that he should be so, that he should stress the *dura lex sed lex*, the advantage of even imperfect laws over the absence of any law whatsoever. But his "certainty" can be only a comparative one. New values may emerge, challenging the existing order and clamouring for recognition. Other legal orders exist, based upon different assumptions and yet securing the allegiance of men. Or it may be that the "certainty" of the legal order is inadequate, that even the most "complete" and "exclusive" system of laws cannot foresee all possible emergencies.[1] In all such cases the student of law is made painfully

[1] This is particularly interesting in the case of Continental code-law, where express reservations are made for the possibility that neither positive law nor custom may provide a sufficient basis for decision, and the necessity of recourse to the " general principles of law " or other criteria is clearly indicated (e.g., *Swiss Civil Code*, Art. 1 ; *Italian Civil Code*, Art. 3 *Disp. Prel.*, etc.).

aware of the limits of his "certainty". This is the reason why the claims of natural law are to him so disturbing. He is made to realize the unceasing interplay of "values" and "norms", of *verum* and *certum*. He is forced to admit that the ultimate ground of the validity of law can lie only in the values which it embodies.

I am, of course, fully aware that the notion of natural law can be acceptable to the jurist only inasmuch as it offers an instrument for the better understanding of legal phenomena, a means of sharpening the tools which he employs. But, as I have already remarked, certain recent developments of legal theory are in this respect particularly instructive. We have seen the jurist recognize that "law" does not necessarily coincide with the law of the State. We have found him aware that his "choice" is a purely arbitrary one, a matter of ideology —and indeed how could he deny the close links which make modern legal positivism a typical outcome of nineteenth century State worship? Yet, on the other hand, we have found the jurist conceding that there is no logical impossibility in the "scientific" construction of any given legal material, be it the law of the State or the law of the Church, the laws of primitive societies or those of the international community— not to speak of the innumerable other laws which in the variety of their intercourse men have come to consider as binding, and indeed "rigorously obey". In all such cases the student of law is led back to the basic questions which inspired former discussions about the nature of law.

The abandonment of the "voluntarist" conception of law in modern jurisprudence, the very change in juridical terminology of which the substitution of "norm" for "precept" or "command" is a clear indication,[1] both seem to point towards a better appraisal of certain notions with which natural law theorists have made us familiar. Such are the notions that the primary function of law is not to command but to qualify, and that legal valuations partake of a logical as well as of a practical character. These notions had been fully displayed by the theorists of the law they stressed that law of nature when

---

[1] See above, p. 105.

is an act of the intellect besides and before being an act of the will. It is fascinating to see these old notions re-emerge, in modern legal theory, in the form of the analogy, to which I have already called attention, between law and language.

If law be considered primarily as a "sign" or an indication of a quality, language and law cannot fail to appear closely similar. The parallel is further confirmed by the similarity between the work of the jurist and that of the grammarian and linguist. Both purport to formulate the general rules applying to the use of certain symbols or signs which men use for qualifying certain given situations. Both lead to an increasing degree of abstraction and "formalism", and are thus liable to the same fallacy of forgetting that the rules which they lay down have a meaning only in so far as they refer to a living reality. Grammars and dictionaries, phonology and morphology do not make a language. Jurisprudence is unable to say the final word about law.[1]

The lesson of natural law, if it were to be recalled in this connection, would, I suppose, be simply to remind the jurist of his own limitations. No philological effort will ever be able to explain a work of art. Nor can jurisprudence reach the ultimate core of law and account for its existence. The lesson of natural law is that the logical character of law does not necessarily imply a denial that law is a part of ethics. What language is to thought, norms are to values. Ultimately, it is on the basis of these that man makes his choice and determines his action. The transformation of a norm into a command is

[1] The analogy of law and language can be traced back to the Historical school, which developed it in accordance with the Romantic interest in folk-lore and *Sittengeschichte*. The similarity between the work of the grammarian and that of the jurist was to my knowledge first pointed out by B. Croce in an essay on legal philosophy in 1907 ; but references to grammar and grammatical rules have always been frequent among students of law at all times.

The relationship between law and language has recently been approached from an entirely new angle in this country and in the U.S.A. It is mentioned in C. L. STEVENSON's book, *Ethics and Language*, 1946, and discussed in greater detail by G. L. WILLIAMS in "Law Quarterly Review," 1945–46. An excellent contribution to the analysis of legal language has been made by Professor HART (*The Ascription of Responsibility and Rights*, Aristotelian Society, 1949).

essentially a matter of subjective appreciation. Surely there
is no command where there is no obedience.

Here, indeed, is where the moralist will have his word to
say, and will decide whether the old speculations on the nature
of law are entirely superseded. If he be the man of the *verum*
he will not ignore that the certainty for which conscience
craves is not that of transient laws, but that of absolute values.
He will provide such grounds for obedience as are capable of
carrying conviction. But he will also take into account the
unrelenting quest of man to rise above the "letter of the law"
to the realm of the spirit. He will draw the dividing line
between mere conformity to the law and the real value of action,
between the Pharisee and the truly moral man.

I have endeavoured in this book to show how deeply
concerned the theorists of natural law were with these issues.
We ought not to forget the great debt we owe them. They
were the first to explore the ambiguous borderland between
law and morals. They were the first to secure the comparative
independence of the law-giver as well as the inviolable rights
of the individual conscience. They were the first to analyse
the complex interplay of legal and moral obligation, the
mysterious process by which the truly honest man abides by
the law and yet is free from its bondage. We must be careful
before we reject their eloquent plea that law is a part of ethics.
We must ask ourselves whether there is not a permanent
element of truth in their contention that law and morals are
closely intertwined and yet fundamentally different ; that it
is from the idea of the good that all "normative" judgments
proceed, and yet that the essence of moral experience is
freedom.

I know of no better description of this process than that
given by Kant in a famous passage which I would like to quote
as the conclusion of this essay. Kant's ethics may appear, and
probably are, not entirely immune from a "legalistic" bias.
But nobody had a clearer grasp than Kant had of the incom-
mensurable difference between legality and morality.

"A perfectly good will . . . [cannot] . . . be conceived as
necessitated to act in conformity with law, since of itself, in

accordance with its subjective constitution, it can be determined only by the concept of the good. Hence for the *divine* will, and in general for a *holy* will, there are no imperatives : '*I ought*' is here out of place, because '*I will*' is already of itself necessarily in harmony with the law. Imperatives are in consequence only formulæ for expressing the relation of objective laws of willing to the subjective imperfection of the will of this or that rational being—for example, of the human will" (KANT, *The Moral Law* (*Groundwork of the Metaphysic of Morals*), transl. by H. J. Paton, p. 81).

This point where values and norms coincide, which is the ultimate origin of law and at the same time the beginning of moral life proper, is, I believe, what men for over two thousand years have indicated by the name of natural law.

INDEX